Three Kingdoms on the
Roof of the World

Three Kingdoms on the Roof of the World

Bhutan, Nepal, Ladakh

Text and photographs by
ROBERT Z. APTE, Ph.D.

PARALLAX PRESS
BERKELEY, CALIFORNIA

PARALLAX PRESS
P.O. Box 7355
Berkeley, CA 94707

LIBRARY OF CONGRESS CATALOGING-IN-PUBLICATION DATA
Apte, Robert Z.
    Three kingdoms on the roof of the world : Bhutan, Nepal, and Ladakh / text and photographs by Robert Z. Apte.
        p.   cm.
    Includes bibliographical references (p.) and index,
    ISBN 0-938077-33-3 : $35.00
    1. Bhutan.   2. Nepal.   3. Ladakh (India)   I. Title.   II. Title: 3 kingdoms on the roof of the world.
    DS491.4.A68   1990
    954'.00943—dc20   90-7710
                                                                            CIP

ENDPAPERS: *Mani wall in sea of prayer flags at a pass leading from Thimpu to Eastern Bhutan.*

PAGE i: *Temple squares and temple sculpture are the playgrounds for the young. This young fellow is holding on to the trunk of the Hindu elephant god Ganesh-Bhaktapur.*

FRONTISPIECE: *Chorten Chora, Tashi Yangtze—Eastern Bhutan.*

FACING PAGE: *Children playing joyously in a field of prayer flags— Eastern Bhutan.*

PHOTOGRAPHY: Robert Z. Apte, with exceptions as noted below
TEXT AND JACKET DESIGN: Paula Schlosser
COMPOSITION: Wilsted & Taylor
PRINTING AND BINDING: Everbest Printing Company, Hong Kong, through Asia print/Everbest U.S.A.

ADDITIONAL PHOTOGRAPHY CREDITS: page 12, Dr. Edward Bernbaum; page 120, John Page; back jacket flap, Sara Mathews.

MAP OF THE THREE KINGDOMS: page 126.

Printed in Hong Kong

10   9   8   7   6   5   4   3   2   1

To my Evelyn,
who was beside me every step
culminating in this photo essay,
and to Ann and Horace Sheldon,
who shared with us the wonders
of the magnificent Himalayas.

Chorten Cora, a sacred spot in far eastern Bhutan, where a large, raucous festival is held annually.

CONTENTS

FOREWORD

I MET ROBERT APTE eight years ago in Ladakh and, during the intervening years, I've been greatly impressed by his appreciation and concern for the people of the Himalayas.

When I first visited Ladakh in 1975, it was one of the few indigenous cultures on the planet that had not been affected by the process of Westernization. People lived much as they had for 2,000 years, enjoying a remarkably high standard of living, despite extremely limited resources.

I've been privileged to spend much of the last 15 years in the Himalayas, mostly in Ladakh, but with prolonged periods in Bhutan and Nepal. The magic is still there—the tranquility, the color, the smiles. But so is the threat. Increasingly exposed to the pressures of the modern world, these three kingdoms face the real danger of environmental and cultural breakdown.

Fortunately there are efforts throughout the Himalayas to conserve and protect this unique environment. In some cases serious damage has already occurred, but from La-dakh in the West to Bhutan in the East, there are now widespread initiatives, at both grassroots and government levels, to secure a sustainable future. This book supports those efforts.

The beautiful photographs draw us right into the heart of the traditional culture, giving us glimpses not only of the magnificent landscape, art, and architecture, but of everyday village life. This documentation is of particular value for a part of the world that is changing so rapidly. It is not, however, just a pretty picture book. These photographs testify to the existence of cultures in which people live at peace with themselves, with each other, and with the Earth. The text offers the reader insights into more contemporary issues and points to some of the challenges that lie ahead. Robert Apte's book is a welcome addition to the literature on the Himalayas.

HELENA NORBERG-HODGE
Founder and Director, Ladakh Project
Leh, Ladakh
July 1990

The ancient royal palace of Leh, with the town clustered around its base.

PREFACE

BEFORE LEAVING ON MY last visit to the Himalayas, a close friend asked me if I planned to climb Kathmandu. Since Kathmandu is the capital of Nepal, one of the great historical sites in Asia, I had to politely tell her I wouldn't be climbing that mountain. I have always been astonished that even in my city, Berkeley, a university community and the center of a large international trekking industry, so few people have a clear notion of the diversity of physical and human environments that lie within the great Himalayan Range.

My professional background is in the social sciences, and I have always had a strong interest in visiting and observing remote cultures. In 1977, my wife and I embarked upon an exploration of the Hindu Kush in Pakistan. Invigorated by the grandeur of the high snowcapped peaks and the rich human encounters along the trail, and having overcome a debilitating back injury, I vowed to see as much of this area of the Earth as possible. Especially interesting to me was entering small, distinct ethnic enclaves, each separated by short distances, but also by distant historical events that brought each group to their fragile mountain habitats. Since that time I have often returned to the Himalayas visiting cultures remote from one another as the Pamir Mountain tribes in Tajikistan, U.S.S.R., and the nomadic Brukpa people living in far eastern Bhutan.

Considered sacred by the Hindus, Machhupuchhare, or Fishtail Mountain, is off limits to the climbers.

Holy man chanting as he twirls a prayer wheel.

Nothing less than an encyclopedia would be required to describe fully the range of Himalayan societies and the milieux in which they live. However, I have chosen to write this book about Bhutan, Nepal, and Ladakh because they represent fascinating and contrasting examples of extremes in culture and environment along this 1,500-mile sweep of the rugged Himalayas. Knowledge of their geography, history, cultures, and religions gives the reader a broad overview of the range of the Himalayas. The images were chosen to provide the reader with lively visual presentation of the contrasts among the three areas, as well as many noteworthy similarities, especially the religious beliefs held in common, inspired by the lofty presence of the mighty mountains.

This book is being written during a time when these "kingdoms" are in a state of flux, buffeted by forces within and without. But when has this not been the case? Squeezed between often unfriendly giants, India and China, they have always had to be reactive to their external pressures. Indeed, during the writing of this book, significant changes have taken place within each kingdom.

In the Fall of 1987, based on its King's desire to protect the country's cultural heritage, Bhutan was closed to outside visitors except for trekkers and climbers who were given permits to visit the more remote areas. In 1989, major rioting took place between Buddhists and Muslims in Leh, Ladakh, sparked by a long-standing power struggle and ethnic tensions, causing the region to be temporarily closed to visitors. Shortly before we went to press, in the Spring of 1990, extraordinary demonstrations and strikes held against the Nepalese government by previously excluded political groups persuaded the King to allow the development of a multiparty democracy and free elections.

If *Three Kingdoms on the Roof of the World* provides the reader with a greater knowledge of this fascinating, diverse, and changing part of the world, and even spurs a few to experience the Himalayas directly, my mission will have been accomplished.

ROBERT Z. APTE, PH.D.
Berkeley, California
July 1, 1990

Acknowledgments

A BOOK OF THIS NATURE required the help of many people. Without the enthusiastic support of family, colleagues, and friends, I could never have persisted these past several years to bring it to completion. I especially want to thank everyone who read and commented on the work and viewed the images, as thousands of photos were finally reduced to 144. Among those who patiently viewed my Himalayan images was Mr. David Featherstone, Director of Publications of the Friends of Photography, San Francisco.

I especially want to thank the staff of Inner Asia for making my trips to Bhutan possible, and for providing an opportunity to visit the far reaches of that country; His Excellency Mr. Paul Matthews, Resident Representative of the United Nations in Bhutan, for sharing his knowledge of the country and its struggles with modernization; Miss Dachen Tsering of Bhutan for her kind assistance in teaching me a smattering of the Dzonkga language, which was so helpful in forming close relations with the Bhutanese people; Dr. Ed Kelly, formerly of the Bhutan Ministry of Education, for sharing in depth his understanding of the social life and culture of this elusive kingdom; and Dr. Judith Justice, long familiar with Bhutan, for reading and commenting on parts of my manuscript. To Dr. Edwin Bernbaum I would like to express my gratitude for the contribution of his excellent photograph of Mt. Chomolari that appears on page 12 of this book. Special appreciation is extended to His Majesty the King of Bhutan, Jigme Singye Wangchuck, who has, through his sound policies and fine judgment, made it possible to preserve the Bhutanese culture and protect its lands.

Since my first visit to Nepal in 1977, numerous people have contributed to my understanding of this unique country, including the many Sherpas who guided me into remote areas and the academics who have helped me become aware of the richness and diversity of the country. All of these I wish to thank. Also my appreciation goes to the University of California Center for Southeast Asian Studies for the interest it has shown in Nepalese society. The conference it organized in Berkeley in 1985, with highly knowledgeable Nepalese and American academics, added significantly to my understanding of the contemporary problems of the country. Outstanding among the participants was Dr. Bahadur Bista, of Tribhuvan University, Nepal, who provided a most penetrating understanding of the acculturation process.

Regarding Ladakh, my appreciation is extended to the staff of the Ladakh Project, who hosted my stay in that region of the Himalayas. Through their efforts it was possible to gain a valuable understanding of the Ladakhi culture and current crises. Special thanks go to Ms. Helena Norberg-Hodge and Mr. John Page, who aided me in obtaining a better understanding of the important ecological and social issues affecting all three of the countries. Using Ladakh as an example of a land with few resources, they have pointed out a path, using a range of old and new technologies, that demonstrates well the opportunities for appropriate development. Mr.

Page provided the beautiful photograph of the Ladakhi women wearing their peraks on page 120. I wish also to thank Mr. Peter Goering for sharing with me the difficult-to-obtain information about the governance of Ladakh and for reviewing parts of this text.

When the initial concept of this book began to turn into a reality, a number of individuals greatly contributed to its final production. Ms. Helen Berliner played a significant role through the application of her wide knowledge of the Buddhist religion and her fine editorial skills. Paula Schlosser, the art editor and designer of this book, brought great pleasure to me in the final phases of the project. With her enthusiastic support, advice, and creative efforts this book, thanks to her, has become much more than a sum of all its parts.

Finally, I wish to thank Mr. Arnold Kotler of Parallax Press, for having the vision to see the usefulness of a book of this nature, and for promoting its publication.

The Tangboche Monastery with Mt. Ama Dablan in the background is situated not far below the base of Mt. Everest—both easterners and westerners alike are in awe with the spirituality of its environs.

With eyes that see all, the crown of the Great Stupa at Swayambunath can be from observed from across the Kathmandu Valley.

The Three Kingdoms: An Overview

THE LAND

BHUTAN, NEPAL, AND LADAKH are part of the Great Himalayan mountain range, which stretches 1,500 miles from end to end and ascends to heights of over 29,000 feet. Two mighty rivers, the Indus and the Brahmaputra, arise in Tibet near the sacred Mount Kailash, and course to the eastern and western ends of the range before emptying into the sea. Along the way, these rivers and their tributaries flow through the three kingdoms, supporting, and at times destroying, life. Fossils and sedimentary deposits indicate that these awe-inspiring landscapes were once under the ocean, formed during the course of millions of years by massive glaciers and land erosion. Geologists theorize that the Great Himalayas came into existence when tectonic forces to the south caused a violent crumpling of the earth's crust, and the flat subcontinent of India collided with the land mass to the north, forcing the extensive range upwards. Subsequent movement and the melting of glaciers cut deep valleys through which torrents of sediment washed onto the Plains of India.

Although 1,500 miles long, the Himalayan range is rarely more than sixty miles wide. Rectangular in shape, it stretches from the northwest to the southeast, so that Ladakh, in the west, is 10° farther north than Bhutan, in the east. Significant differences in climate and vegetation result from this variation in latitude. Precipitation levels vary as well, making for more variation in climate and vegetation. The monsoon, the area's major weather system, moves in a northwesterly direction. It starts earlier and lasts two months longer in the east than the west, so that Bhutan gets significantly more rainfall than Nepal or Ladakh. Like Tibet, Ladakh and the Dolpo region of Nepal are hidden behind high mountains that further deprive them of the moisture from the monsoon. The average rainfall in the capital cities of Bhutan, Nepal, and Ladakh is, respectively: Thimpu, 90 inches; Kathmandu, 43 inches; and Leh, 2 inches. These differences in latitude and precipitation profoundly affect the kinds of habitations, agriculture, and economies of the three kingdoms, and significantly shape their cultures.

The flora and fauna of the Great Himalayan range include species from Europe, China, and Japan. In the higher elevations to the west, where rainfall is abundant, there are many European plant species, including coniferous and deciduous trees. Where the forests have not been destroyed by humans, species similar to those in Switzerland flourish—even the celebrated Alpine *edelweiss* can be seen at 9,000 feet in the western sectors. Many Mediterranean species are found at lower altitudes, and at the lowest elevations, where the climate is hot, the flora are similar to that of tropical India. The eastern parts of the Himalayas sustain plants and trees more commonly seen in Japan and China, including rhododendron, bamboo, and magnolia. At elevations between 6,000 and 8,000 feet, orchids cling to trees in great abundance and variety.

Because they are adjacent to the land masses of Europe, China, Malaysia, and Africa, the Himalayas are home to perhaps the greatest variety of mammals and reptiles in the world, including the elephant, one-horned rhinoceros, tiger, leopard, snow leopard, Himalayan black bear, lesser panda, a great variety of primates, as well as the python, cobra, and crocodile.

RELIGION

Because there has been such a steady flow of religious teachers and practitioners across the frontiers of the three kingdoms, the streams of religious beliefs found here are quite similar. Early on, Buddhism was incorporated into the *Bon*, the indigenous religion of all three kingdoms. In the Kathmandu Valley, Buddhism and Hinduism became closely affiliated. Later, *tantric*, or *vajrayana*, Buddhist rituals were added to the religious mix, and ceremonies today often include aspects of all these traditions. The administration of religious institutions also goes beyond national boundaries, and Bhutan, for example, operates monastic enclaves as far away as Ladakh, while all three kingdoms are closely associated religiously with Tibet.

The rituals of the ancient, animistic religion of Bon, practiced for centuries in all three kingdoms, included ablution, circumambulation of sacred spots, purification, animal sacrifice, and in earlier times even human sacrifice. Bon rituals can still be observed in isolated areas of Nepal and in remote valleys of southern Bhutan. In the ninth century, Bon was established as the state religion of Tibet, but by the end of the first millennium, Buddhism had gained ascendancy, and many Bon rituals were incorporated into it. Scholars trace a number of Buddhist symbols and beliefs to the indigenous practices of Bon.

Gautama Buddha was born in the sixth century B.C.E. in Lumbini, Nepal, and died around the year 488 B.C.E. He came from a royal family, and his early life can be described as hedonistic, or indulgent. But as he grew older and witnessed the sufferings and tragedies of life, he renounced his title and claim to power and wealth, and became an itinerant monk practicing austerities and meditation. As a result of these practices, he attained enlightenment and became known as the *Buddha*, "the one who is awake." After his awakening, he travelled throughout northeastern India during the course of forty-five years, delivering his profound message, and sowing the seeds of what developed into the Buddhist monastic system.

The Buddha's perspective on life was a prescription for healthy and sane living according to human wisdom principles, rather than an explanation of man's relationship to God or the cosmos. Meditating on the tragedies of life, the Buddha mapped out a path to help individuals achieve peace and come to grips with the painful aspects of existence. When he died at the age of eighty, having attained a heavenly bliss known as *nirvana*, numerous disciples gathered around him, and over the course of centuries they and their disciples carried on his teaching.

The goal of Buddhism is to bring individuals to a state of peace and insight through the "Eightfold Path" of Right Views, Right Aspirations, Right Speech, Right Conduct, Right Livelihood, Right Effort, Right Mindfulness, and Right Concentration. Although rooted in a particular cultural and historical perspective, the Eightfold Path addresses a timeless human condition. The Buddha held that humans suffer because of their countless desires and attachments, and that by loosening the bonds of these attachments, they can attain inner peace.

The concept of *karma*, which says that the quality of an individual's life is largely a result of past deeds, was adopted by the Buddhists from previously existing beliefs. The drive to improve one's karma explains much of the daily behavior of Buddhists, who perform good deeds and fastidiously observe rituals in order to gain "merit." The Buddha also incorporated meditation practices, including various contemplative techniques used by the yogis of India since ancient times, into his path to enlightenment.

The Buddha made no claim to divinity. Originally the guidance he offered was not even thought of as a religion, but within a millennium, Buddhism became institutionalized and evolved many branches and schools, each with its own specialized set of teachings and rituals.

The earliest form of Buddhism, the Theravadin school (teachings of the elders), is most faithful to the forms and practices introduced by the Buddha. It is still practiced today in Burma, Thailand, Sri Lanka, Cambodia, Laos, and parts of Vietnam. The schools known as Mahayana, or "Greater Vehicle," date back to the first century B.C.E., and are prevalent today in eastern Asia, including Japan, Korea, China, and parts of Vietnam. These schools emphasize the possibility that greater numbers of beings can attain enlightenment, while the saint, or *bodhisattva*, delays his or her own salvation until everyone else succeeds.

In the kingdoms of Bhutan, Nepal, and Ladakh, Vajrayana, the "Indestructible Vehicle," also called Lamaism or Tantrism, is the dominant form of Buddhism. Vajrayana Buddhism developed in India and came to the Himalayas during the sixth century, combining the Mahayana aspiration to liberate all sentient beings from suffering, with the ritualistic practices of Bon.

Over the centuries an extensive pantheon of tantric deities has evolved. Each represents one aspect of the personality of the Buddha. Practitioners invoke and identify with these deities through offerings, "magical" rituals, and meditation practices. One theme that recurs in tantrism is that there are two major forces in the universe, male and female, whose interaction creates the drama of life. The male aspect contains the notion of activity and skillful means; the female, the notion of space and wisdom. Internally, the female energy exists in the left side of the body, with the male force on the right side. Through yogic exercise, the practitioner can enter a blissful state of nonduality.

The term Hinduism covers a multitude of religious beliefs that developed in India thousands of years ago. It includes the caste system, which dictates hierarchical interclass relationships, diet, dress, occupation, and specific religious practices. The *Upanishads* are the sacred scriptures of Hinduism, teaching the *Dharma*, the way to spiritual enlightenment. Hindu Dharma is an ancient prescription for righteous living, an acceptance of life within one's caste, and a respect for all life. The eating of meat, for instance, is forbidden.

Hinduism appeals to the senses, as music, dance, and even the production of mellifluous perfumes are central to the devotional observances. The religion abounds in complex allegories through which high-minded ideals and morals are espoused. The promise of a better future existence is held out for all through the belief that one can improve one's lot by performing good deeds. Furthermore, the notion of karma explains and justifies one's current situation; whether one is miserable or fortunate, low caste or high, is a result of one's own behavior in a prior existence. Although a later development, the caste system became an important part of the daily life of Hindus. Although illegal today in India, it remains an important part of Hindu culture.

The major Hindu deities are the triumvirate of Brahma, Vishnu, and Shiva. Brahma is believed to be the creator of the universe, Vishnu the preserver, and his counterpart, Shiva, the destroyer. Vishnu and Shiva also manifest in many other forms such as the gods Rama and Krishna. Innumerable deities and practices vary from village to village, but certain underlying beliefs and customs are common to all. The Brahmins, for instance, have been the priests and scholars of the faith from earliest times. When they were driven out of India during the Muslim invasions, they carried their Hindu faith into Nepal. Although many are now farmers, they still hold the high status of priests in the caste system.

ART

In India during the first millennium of this era, Buddhist and Hindu art flourished. The temples and shrines were richly adorned with sculpture and paintings. During the Moghul invasions, most of this art was destroyed, but the Hindus and Buddhists who traveled north from India into the Himalayas, spread their artistic traditions.

Because of the remoteness of the Himalayan kingdoms, the sacred art from India first appeared in the centers that lay along the caravan routes. Here small metal and stone sculptures of the Buddha were brought by traders and monks en route to Kashmir, Ladakh, and Lhasa. Later, knowledge of painting, sculpture, and the working of metals penetrated from India into the Kathmandu Valley, which became a center for the creation of sacred art. The extraordinary skills of Kathmandu's artists and craftsmen spread throughout the region, and the three king-

doms, less affected by the Muslim destruction than India, retained a wonderful legacy of masterpieces of pre-Moghul art. Works from this period and subsequent phases still exist in sacred buildings throughout the region. As Madanjeet Singh, who surveyed Himalayan art for UNESCO, points out, "Ancient art preserved in the Himalayan monasteries and temples reflects great periods in the history of Asia and the world in the same way as the ruins of Pompeii give an insight into the civilization of Rome at its height."

Although these sacred works took many forms, all reflect the spirituality of the artists who created them in the shadows of the great mountains. In Nepal, where Hinduism became the dominant faith, statues and paintings of Vishnu, Brahma, Shiva, and their various manifestations dominate courtyards and temples, modeled after the traditional styles developed in India. Indian art of the Gupta Period (fourth to sixth century C.E.) was the first major influence in Nepal, and it has varied little over the centuries.

The earliest representations of the Buddha were created in Swat, now part of Pakistan, during the Kushan Empire (50 B.C.E. to 210 C.E.). This *Gandharan* style of art was strongly influenced by the Persian and Roman-Hellenistic Empires. This style developed from the reciprocal east-west exchange of ideas and artifacts that traveled the Silk Route between China and Greece. As a result, the Buddha was given an oval-shaped face, a long Aryan nose, and a flowing toga. This western style of sculpture, so different from the sculpture of the period in India, had a profound and far-reaching effect on Buddhist art.

Buddhist art in the Himalayan region took many forms. *Thangka* painting was, and still is, the most popular form used to depict the Buddha's teachings. Painted in scroll form on linen, thangkas could be easily rolled up and carried from place to place as a kind of portable shrine. They became the visual focus of worship in the temples, monasteries, and homes of the common people.

One subject of thangka painting is the representation of *mandalas*, and another is the portrayal of enlightened beings. Mandalas are used to aid visualization in meditation. They are composed of "palaces," or central squares with four gates expanding out to the four cardinal directions—north, south, east, and west. The central image is often the Buddha or a manifestation of the Buddha. The fringe is generally composed of miniature scenes emphasizing the principles of the faith. The precise form of a mandala is determined by specific *sadhana* liturgies and scriptures. The artist's creative talents are expressed in the rendering of the details and peripheral scenes.

Paintings of enlightened beings are also quite stylized, but vary greatly in size and content and allow for more creativity than mandalas. The central figure can be surrounded by a number of miniature scenes, often arranged into "zones" representing biographical events or themes of the Buddhist Dharma. The lofty, cloud-engulfed, snow-capped Himalayas figure prominently in most of these scenes. Like the mandala paintings, thangkas are religious "tools" to evoke a specific inspiration and energy in the observer, and to connect him or her with that inspiration as an inner reality transcending the reality of the material world.

Another traditional art form found in temples and monasteries are wall paintings depicting the life of the Buddha, Guru Padmasambhava, who is said to have brought Buddhism from India to Tibet, or one of the numerous bodhisattvas. Like European frescoes, they are painted on walls that have been primed with undercoatings of emulsion and then polished. The colors used here are the same natural colors used in the thangkas.

Part One
BHUTAN

A young woman in from the fields carrying sheaths of rice.

Young monks hanging new prayer flags at a promontory leading to Tak Sang monastery.

Tak Sang is an ancient monastery built upon a steep precipice. It is the site where Guru Padmasambhava meditated in a cave.

The Land

BHUTAN IS KNOWN TO its people as *Druk Yul*, the "Land of the Thunder Dragon." The drama of its name is reflected in the grandeur of its landscape. Easternmost of the three kingdoms, it is surrounded by India on the west, south, and east, and by Chinese-occupied Tibet to the north. The Chomolhari range of the Himalayas, rising to over 24,000 feet and continually covered with glaciers and snow, are the northern border of Bhutan. A number of passes in this range open onto the impressive Chumbu Valley of Tibet, which historically has been so important to Bhutan's commercial, cultural, and religious development. Massive mountains also extend along the border of the Indian states of Arunchal Pradesh to the east and Sikkim to the west. The southern border of Bhutan lies along the Gangetic plains where, from no more than 1,000 feet, foothills rise immediately and dramatically into mountain highlands.

The topography of Bhutan in relation to India and Tibet can be compared to a clenched fist lying palmside down on a table. The top of the hand sloping up to the knuckles is a high plateau, the Chumbu Valley of Tibet; the knuckles, a range of massive mountains; the grooves between the fingers, the deep valleys of Bhutan descending steeply to a flat surface, the Gangetic plains of India to the south.

It is said that the boundary between Bhutan and India was determined by rolling a ball downhill: wherever the ball stopped rolling, India began. The border region of foothills, though less than 200 miles in width, is still the widest part of the country. Like the Terai in Nepal, it is a sticky, tropical region, mostly impenetrable bamboo, chestnut, and oak forest, thick with tropical plants and fruit trees. To the east, along the banks of the Manas River, wild elephants, tigers, rhinoceros, and buffalo still roam. Where the river breaks through this torrid region, clusters of small communities earn their livelihood from agriculture and from trade with India. These extremely fertile areas are referred to as the Duars. Phuntsholing, a small border town with a mixture of Bhutanese, Nepalese, and Indian residents, is the southern gateway to Bhutan, and it is through here that most foot and vehicular traffic passes en route to the highlands.

At higher altitudes, ranging from 4,000 to 10,000 feet, are eight major valleys: Haa, Paro, Thimpu, Punaka, Tongsa, Bumthang, Kuru, and Kulong. The majority of the Bhutanese population lives in this inner Himalayan region. Some of these valleys are broad, some quite narrow (see photograph, page 10). Rivers thunder through them from northern glaciers, their currents too swift to be navigated. Frequent landslides and erosion make overland travel unpredictable. It can take more than a week to travel across the country by car, despite the recently built system of paved roads. The author counted fifty landslides in eastern Bhutan in a one-hour drive.

The valleys in the west have heavier rainfall than those in the east. On the whole, Bhutan experiences much more precipitation than Nepal or Ladakh, as the monsoons lay their blankets of rain and snow there first. The combina-

Gantey Valley, in western Bhutan, is at about 11,000 feet and is an example of an agriculturally rich valley.

tion of adequate rainfall, agreeable climate, and fertile alluvial soils have endowed Bhutan with the richest agriculture in the Himalayas. Planting of crops in the valleys is intense. Farmers sow the land in picturesque patterns, sculpting the terrain into neatly contoured terraces of corn, rice, wheat, and buckwheat. Fruit orchards and vegetable gardens abound. In the lower valleys such as Punaka and Mongar, bananas, citrus, and other tropical fruits are also grown.

Surrounding the valleys one finds magnificent conifer forests, rich with spruce, blue pine, fir, juniper, and hemlock. Gigantic Rhododendron trees, up to forty feet high, are commonplace at higher altitudes. The sub-alpine scenery of the inner Himalayas, its hillside pastures dotted with grazing animals and adorned with uniquely styled Bhutanese houses, looks remarkably like Switzerland. Unlike arid Ladakh, or Nepal with its vanishing forest cover and topsoil, Bhutan is richly verdant. It is a country where the grand plan of nature has not been despoiled by humans. Although there is abundant agriculture, in fact the percentage of cultivated land is exceedingly small.

In the northern zone, the mountains rise above the clouds to form the Great Himalayas. Soaring more than 24,000 feet, these giants serve as a fortress against Tibet. Mount Gangker Punsum, the "White Glacier of the Spiritual Brothers," is the highest at 24,600 feet. The more famous, sacred Mount Chomolari, sits at 23,997 feet (page 12). This area is a mass of peaks and glaciers, twisting and turning into larger and larger pathways for the thunderous rivers rushing down to the sea. Although a few yak herdsmen do ascend the lower heights for summer grazing, this secluded corner of the world is an area of untamed beauty—miniature plant life peeking up through melting summer snow, blue sheep, takin, and musk deer grazing on the slopes, and snow leopard and Himalayan bear still roaming the land.

Although potential mineral wealth and a great opportunity for the development of hydroelectric power exist, only a few small power stations have been established and there is no aggressive policy for natural resource development. Very few natural resources are exported, principally some timber to India, Bhutan's main trading partner.

Even though Bhutan is remarkably self-sufficient, there is still a desire for hard currency to purchase medical and manufactured products, so the country has recently extended the use of its mountainous areas to trekkers and

This bridge by Tashigong is an example of an old chain which is still in use.

The sacred mountain of Chomolari situated at 23,997 feet.

mountaineers in limited numbers. It is hoped that this policy can be administered carefully so that fragile ecological areas will be protected from overuse. So far the impact of imported western products has been minimal and limited to only a few small towns.

The lack of economic development in Bhutan is due not only to the difficult geographic location, but also to a strict historical policy of self-imposed isolation. Under both the previous and current kings, this policy has been moderated and Bhutan is now an active member in the community of nations. But the outside forces that might disrupt the cultural and socioeconomic equilibrium of the country are strictly controlled. Should it become necessary to close its borders as in the past, Bhutan could continue to manage its resources wisely and become self-sufficient again.

People of Bhutan

Earthquakes and fires have repeatedly destroyed any documents that could have revealed details of Bhutan's past. Historians have had to piece together information about the original inhabitants of the land, most likely an Indo-Mongoloid race which practiced the Bon religion. Over time, successive waves of migration came from the north and the south. Even now, however, small tribal groups of ancient origins remain in isolated valleys where they continue to practice their ancient indigenous religion.

The majority of Bhutanese today are descendents of the *Drukpas*, or *Ngalops*, whose ancestors arrived from Tibet in the ninth century. They occupied the western valleys of Haa, Paro, Thimpu, Punaka, and Bumthang. The eastern valleys are populated by the *Sharchop* people, who most likely are descendents of the original inhabitants. In the easternmost valley of Sakteng resides the *Brukpa* tribe, a group related to the *Mons* of northeastern India. The Brukpas are a Mongoloid race and also speak a Tibeto-Burmese language (pages 14, 15). Due to the arid climate and infertile land, their standard of living is considerably lower than that of western Bhutan. Some of these people are semi-nomadic herdsmen who tend livestock at higher altitudes.

An important minority in Bhutan are the Nepalese who migrated there in the nineteenth century to find land and work. They are most heavily concentrated in the south, where they have become farmers and traders. Because Bhutan is underpopulated, with approximately one

Bringing apples to market, a scene at the confluence of the Mo and Po rivers.

A Brukpa family at Tashigong, coming to the village at market day.

Bartering or selling produce along the way, a ubiquitous activity.

million inhabitants, the Nepalese are readily granted citizenship. Today many Nepalese and Indian laborers work under contract on the construction of the highway system and hydroelectric projects.

Language is a complex problem in Bhutan. With the major valleys separated from one another by several days' walk, languages and dialects differ considerably from place to place. Even among the peoples of Tibetan origin, who share social customs and religious beliefs, the generations have produced distinct local dialects, and people from neighboring valleys do not understand one another. Few understand Tibetan. In addition, the Sharchops and the Nepalese speak totally different languages. In the

1960s *Dzongkha*, the "language of the fortress," was selected as the national language of Bhutan, related to ancient Tibetan. Dzongkha is spoken throughout the country by government workers, and is used in the monasteries and taught, along with English, to Bhutanese school children. Still, Dzongkha lacks wide acceptance throughout the kingdom, and English is generally spoken only by the educated classes.

Bhutan is a country the size of Switzerland, with one-seventh the population. Compared to other Asian countries, Bhutan is quite sparsely populated and, unlike Nepal, it has no cities. The two largest towns, Paro and Thimpu, are little more than overgrown villages. Thimpu

Bhutanese youth dressed in the local school uniform.

The Royal Bhutanese Dance School Director's wife.

is the capital, with a population of 20,000, and this growth has been relatively recent (page 16).

Strategically located at the head of each major valley are the formidable *dzongs*, massive stone structures which served as both fortresses and monasteries. In earlier times they were impenetrable. The dzong at Tongsa was situated so that travelers had to pass through it to go on to the next valley. Today, the dzongs still house the monasteries and also serve as the administrative headquarters for each region. Clustered around the base of each major dzong is a small community such as Paro, Thimpu, Wangdi Podrang, Tongsa, Jakar, Mongar, and Tashigong. The people living in these communities are associated with government, trade, or the monasteries.

The majority of Bhutanese people are peasants who make their living by farming or raising livestock. Scattered over the fertile valleys is a mosaic of well-tended fields (page 18). At altitudes of 2,000 to 10,000 feet, a great variety of crops, such as barley and potatoes, grow in abundance. Above 12,000 feet, the grazing is good and semi-nomadic yak herdsmen make their homes there. Yaks provide wool and leather, a cheese that is a staple of the Bhutanese diet, and meat, which when dried is regarded as a luxury. During the summer months, these nomads live in tents woven from yak hair, and in the winter they move down the mountainsides and stay in primitive, stone huts (pages 17, 19).

In spite of its great variety of languages and ethnic groups, Bhutanese society is unified by its cultural and religious beliefs. Tibetan Buddhism is the main religion, except among the Nepalese who are largely Hindu, and among the small remote groups who still practice the Bon. The Bhutanese do not, however, regard themselves as Tibetan.[1] While they do acknowledge their Tibetan

An ancient watchtower overlooking the fertile Paro Valley, the site of the Bhutanese National Museum.

cultural and spiritual roots, the Bhutanese are thoroughly immersed in their own national identity. This is especially true in western Bhutan among the Drukpas and less prevalent among the Sharchops and other groups in the east.

Cut off from the world geographically and politically, the Bhutanese have become highly self-sufficient behind their closed borders. The extent to which they do not depend upon other countries for food, clothing, and other necessities of life is remarkable. Until recently, almost all of their needs were met within their borders. They enjoy beautiful homespun clothing, sturdy attractive houses, and a rich variety of arts and crafts.

Bhutan's ability to control its own destiny and to defray the negative aspects of development are reflected in statistics. Unemployment, crime, and mental illness are negligible. While infectious diseases still exist, the government

A monk carrying the holy scriptures between monasteries.

Yak meat—a special gourmet delicacy in Bhutan—put out to dry by a woman butcher—Mongar.

Harvesting buckwheat, Bumthang Valley.

has been building a system of regional clinics and public health services, and in recent years, there has been a decline in the rate of infant mortality. Yet, according to the United Nations and other international agencies, Bhutan is ranked among the poorest nations in the world. But this ranking—determined by the gross national product—is

Winnowing buckwheat in the Bumthang Valley, Central Bhutan.

hardly relevant to Bhutanese society, which is not established on a monetary system, exports little, and carries on a miniscule amount of trade with the outside world. The quality of life, as judged by the Bhutanese people themselves and measured in terms of human values, is remarkably rich, not poor.

Gantey Gompa, a typical small village with its gompa on the hill.

A simple dwelling at Gantey Gompa Village.

Punaka Dzong, where the Shabdung, "The One at whose feet one must submit," presided and is entombed.

History of Bhutan

THE HISTORICAL ORIGINS OF the Bhutanese people are to be found only in legends handed down over the centuries. Tragically, the national archives in the old capital of Punaka were destroyed by two major fires in the nineteenth century. Most of the remaining historical documents were later destroyed at the Paro Dzong during an earthquake. Thanks to the recent work of scholars, the ancient tales have been garnered from the oral histories and re-recorded.[2] They tell us of the close relationship between Tibet and Bhutan. Most importantly, they tell of the arrival of Tibetan Buddhism in Bhutan and of the perpetual conflict between the various Buddhist schools struggling to gain hegemony.

Tibet was converted to Buddhism from the indigenous animistic Bon religion by the seventh century. Under the direction of King Srong-btsans Gampo (627–649), Tibetan monks went into Bhutan and built two Buddhist temples as part of a network of ten similar temples established in Tibet. The two temples are still standing and are the earliest evidence of Buddhism in Bhutan.

Over time, Bhutan became a fertile area for the expansion of Tibetan Buddhism. The teachings were carried across the border by lamas coming as missionaries or, at times, as refugees fleeing tyrant kings or bloody conflicts with rival sects,[3] not unlike the recent dissemination of Buddhist teachings by Tibetan monks fleeing from Chinese domination.[4] Over the centuries, many influential Tibetans resettled and held dominant roles in Bhutan. At least one Tibetan king sought refuge in Bhutan. "All

these figures," Michael Aris writes in his 1979 history of Bhutan, "carry the divine aura of kingship and the local inhabitants, yielding to them as subjects, come to partake of that aura in a relationship that is passed down from generation to generation among their descendents."[5]

An important legend, still fervently believed by most Bhutanese, tells of the formal arrival of Buddhism to Bhutan in the early eighth century.[6] At that time the Indian King Sindhu Raja ruled the district of Bumthang in central Bhutan. After the ravages of a long war, the king became gravely ill. He invited Guru Padmasambhava, considered to be an incarnation of the Buddha, to come from India to help him. When Padmasambhava arrived, he immediately went into a cave to meditate, remaining there for seven days and nights. During his meditation, the legend goes, he struggled constantly with evil spirits until they were overcome. Thereupon, the king's health was restored, and he immediately converted to Buddhism. Today the Bhutanese point out Padmasambhava's meditation cave and his footprint, which is implanted in stone there. Many other shrines have been established throughout Bhutan at sites where Padmasambhava is said to have meditated.

Prior to this conquest, Guru Padmasambhava had traveled to Tibet where he established the *Nyingma*, or "Old School," of Tibetan Buddhism—a tradition which flourishes today. As many other lineages and schools developed in Tibet, their teachings were carried over the Himalayas into Bhutan by Tibetan lamas with missionary zeal. Until the seventeenth century, Bhutan was the scene of continuous conflict, even warfare, among the competing sects—the two main contenders being the *Drukpa Kagyu* and the *Lhapa*.

The Drukpa were already firmly established in Bhutan by the twelfth century. They were patronized by the most powerful families, who helped them build numerous monasteries and shrines in the western valleys. In 1616, a young Tibetan Drukpa lama named Ngawang Namgyal (1593–1651) arrived in Bhutan on a pilgrimage. A nobleman and a recognized *tulku*, he expected to be selected as a high lama, and when he was passed over for this position, he fled from Tibet. At the time, Bhutan was no more than a collection of independent warring states. Ngawang Namgyal, with strong support from the Drukpas, began an extraordinary military career which led to the unification of Bhutan and his own reign as king. He was responsible for building the chain of dzongs that top the valleys of western Bhutan, including the Simtoka Dzong (1629), which stands proudly today.

Ngawang Namgyal repelled six separate invasions from Tibet. The last one, in 1644, was against the Dalai Lama, whose army, joined by the Mongols from the north, attempted to invade Bhutan to enforce the teachings of the *Gelug*, or "Yellow Hat," school of Tibetan Buddhism. Ngawang Namgyal overpowered the combined armed forces, and his victory dampened the belief in the invincibility of the Mongols, who had previously rampaged through Central Asia and China with impunity. These wars to defend Bhutan helped consolidate the Bhutanese factions and Ngawang Namgyal's leadership. Before his power was made secure, however, he had to overcome his main adversaries, the five groups of Bhutanese lamas, who furiously opposed the Drukpa school.

Following this victory his reputation was so great that he was given the title of *Shabdung*, the "Supreme Power," or "One at Whose Feet One Must Submit" (page 20).

As king of Bhutan, having unified the country, he set about organizing a "dual theocracy," a system of government in which both religious and lay administrative positions were held by lamas. The civil power was directed by a high-ranking lay leader called a *Deb*, and each of the districts was governed by a *Penlop*. The dzongs were the centers of the districts, and civil matters were administered by *Dzongpons*. For the first time the country had written laws. The successor to the Shabdung would be found by locating his tulku, or reincarnation.

The first Europeans to visit Bhutan came during Ngawang Namgyal's reign. In 1627, two Portuguese Jesuit priests, Cacella and Cabral, made the arduous journey and spent six months there. Their written impressions of Bhutan and of the Shabdung are among the few available accounts of this period. They describe the ruler as gentle and benevolent to his subjects, preferring that any support and contributions by them be given voluntarily. He was tolerant of the Jesuits' religion and would allow them to set up a church and mission.[7] Most importantly, Ngawang Namgyal is remembered for his preservation of the sacred Drukpa Kagyu teachings, rather than for his creation of a lasting government. Many of the religious institutions established by this colorful leader continue in Bhutan today.

At the age of fifty-eight, the Shabdung went into a monastic retreat, passing his authority to the Deb Raja, the lay leader. Shortly thereafter, he died—a fact that was kept a closely guarded secret for over fifty years. Concealing the death of a high lama was not an uncommon practice in Tibet. In this case, it was done to maintain a stable government until the Shabdung's genuine tulku could be located. While his attendants continued to bring him food and his alternates signed his decrees, the people, who regarded him as a saint, did not question his continuous state of meditation. Those who tried to divulge the secret met with mysterious deaths. Coincidentally, the Dalai Lama had died in neighboring Tibet where he, too, continued to "rule" for half a century, sitting in erect meditation posture until the secret of his death was revealed.

The Shabdung's tulku came to power as a minor and was overshadowed by the civilian Deb. The Deb's authority was undermined, in turn, by the Penlops in their dzongs, seeking more autonomy for their districts. From then on, the balance between the central and local governments remained in a state of continual disequilibrium until the system of dual theocracy was finally abolished and a monarchy established in 1907.

During the eighteenth century, Bhutan took control over a neighboring state to the south, Cooch Behar. But in 1773, they clashed with the British, who were also determined to control this Indian province, and in a subsequent battle, the Bhutanese army was overcome by a small British force.[8] With the help of the Tibetan Panchen Lama, a peace treaty was signed which granted the British free trade with Bhutan and cleared their way for trade with Tibet. For the next fifty years, however, there was little activity between the two countries aside from occasional diplomatic missions.

During the late eighteenth century, Bhutan annexed the Duars, the low-lying hill districts, which were part of Assam, and seized power from the Ahom kings. The Duars, with their fertile soil and rich harvest, were especially desirable. In the beginning of the nineteenth century, the Bhutanese took power from the Indian Muslim rulers in the Duar districts further west, on the Bhutan-Bengal border.

By 1826, however, the Bhutanese were once again face to face with the British Colonial Forces, now firmly entrenched along Bhutan's southern border. In 1841, having successfully driven the Burmese out of Assam, the British annexed the Assam Duars from Bhutan. This began a period of intermittent conflict which lasted twenty years, culminating in the Anglo-Bhutanese, or Duar, War of 1864, in which the British successfully took over the Bhutanese forts in Bengal. Following this defeat, the Treaty of Simchula was signed, signaling the beginning of peaceful relations between the two countries. Bhutan lost the Duars, but gained an annual payment of 50,000 rupees from British India and free trade with Britain.

By the end of the nineteenth century, it was clear that the dual theocracy was not working—the tulku was usually too young to rule; the Debs lacked the ability to enforce centralized power, and the Penlops were always sparring for more autonomy. The most powerful Penlops of this era were from Paro in the West and Tongsa in the central district.[9] The present royal dynasty is directly descended from the Penlops of Tongsa (page 25).

By the early twentieth century, the British were eager to renew political and economic relations with Tibet. They were also concerned about the movement of expansionist Russia into this region. Since Bhutan stands directly in the path to Tibet, the British needed to consolidate their relations with the leaders of Bhutan. The Tongsa Penlop, Ugyen Wanchuk, was in favor of relations with Britain, hoping to strengthen his own power internally. The Paro Penlop opposed any alliance with Britain, preferring to maintain good relations with Tibet. In 1903, Lord Curzon, the British Viceroy of India, decided that the way to establish a dominant presence in Tibet was to invade through Bhutan. Ugyen Wangchuk and his army agreed to accompany the British expeditionary force, and together they marched over the rugged mountain passes into Tibet and successfully attacked the fortress at Gyanze. After the battle, a peace treaty was signed between Britain and Tibet, and Ugyen Wangchuk became Sir Wangchuk, knighted by the British Crown.[10]

At home, Ugyen Wangchuk was recognized as the leader who could unite the country and in 1907, representatives of the monastic communities and civil authorities chose him as the *Druk Gyalpo*, "Precious Ruler of the Dragon People." This act ended the dual theocracy and began a new hereditary, monarchical system of govern-

ment. Ugyen Wangchuk ruled until 1926, when his son Jigme Wangchuk succeeded him.

The second Druk Gyalpo died in 1952. Until then Bhutan was still an isolated country, its borders effectively closed to outsiders. The only way into the interior was on foot, and it took a week to reach the capital. The wheel had yet to be introduced, even on toys. As a result of this isolation, age-old beliefs and customs persisted.

Since 1952, beginning with the reign of the third Druk Gyalpo, Jigme Dorje Wangchuk, and continuing with the reign of his son, Jigme Singye Wangchuk, Bhutan has emerged from its cloistered state. Both kings have sponsored controlled and responsible development and resisted forces that would degrade their ancient culture.

Tongsa Dzong Court, a principal Dzong in Central Bhutan, ancestral home of the royal family.

Religion in Bhutan

Pious old man poring over the sacred scriptures.

BUDDHISM, HINDUISM, AND BON are the main religions in Bhutan today. Bon, the ancient, indigenous faith of the Himalayas, is found in the extremely remote villages in the low-lying eastern valleys, among the small clusters of people there descended from the earliest Tibetan inhabitants. While no formal Bon institutions exist, rituals such as divination still survive.[11] Those who practice this faith are fairly isolated from the mainstream of Bhutanese life.

Hinduism is the religious tradition of the many Nepalese who migrated into Bhutan in the last century. Although their beliefs are firmly held and their rituals rigorously followed at home, there are few visible signs of Hindu worship in Bhutan.

Buddhism is the state religion of Bhutan. From the ninth century on, Tibetan lamas went to Bhutan and put down permanent roots there. Many of these religious teachers became powerful leaders, establishing their own small theocratic states. This resulted in a multiplicity of schools, each with its own expressions of the basic Buddhist traditions and doctrines, passed on from teacher to disciple. Some lineages, in fact, could only be continued by a recognized tulku, or reincarnation, of the previous lama. Conflict arose among some of the schools, the most fierce being between the Drukpa and Lhapa sects. In the end, the Drukpa school of the Kagyu lineage became the universal religion of Bhutan.

There are few places in the world where the aura of spirituality pervades the landscape so dramatically as in Bhutan. From the depths of the valleys to the highest

Retired monk continues to live among his colleagues at Gantey Gompa Monastery.

mountain passes, the evidences of deep faith and devotion are ubiquitous. Prayer flags flutter in forests of tree-like poles. Prayer wheels twice as tall as a man are inscribed with the mantra *Om Mani Padme Hum*, "Homage to the Jewel in the Lotus" (page 28). Twirled by devotees or powered by waterwheels, they spin their message tirelessly into the wind. Bridge banners also disseminate that sacred message as they flap briskly in the breeze. Long *mani* walls stretch across fields of grain, and gleaming white *chortens* rise like breasts from rich, dark hills.

The exact origin of the chorten is unknown, although they seem to be derivative from Indian Buddhist *stupas*, or reliquaries. Solid mound-like structures varying in size, they are built according to traditional plan and symbolize the five elements of the Buddhist cosmos—fire, water, earth, air, and ether. Relics of Buddhist saints are placed within each chorten, and it often serves as the central shrine of the village. In Bumthang, a large chorten contains the remains of the previous king, Jigme Dorje Wangchuk. Near Tashiyangsi, the impressive Chorten Cora is the site of pilgrimages and annual festivals. Both the mani walls and chortens are considered holy sites, where the faithful go to gain merit. Pilgrims believe that circumambulating these shrines clockwise while reciting the mantra *Om Mani Padme Hum* will earn them great personal merit.

Dominating each major valley is a hill or ridge topped with a foreboding dzong, many of which house ancient *gompas*, or monasteries. Nearby a traditional *lhakhang*, or temple, may be seen. The Bhutanese people freely con-

Masks and drums hanging on a pillar in preparation for the Wangdi Festival.

Elderly women are often hired to keep large prayer wheels rotating.

tribute the cost and care necessary to maintain these buildings, whose sturdy construction testifies to the population's energetic devotion.

Two of the most famous lhakhangs are Jampe in Bumthang Valley and Kyichu in Paro. Built in the eighth century by the Tibetan King Srong Sam Gampo, Jambe and Kyichu are the oldest lhakhangs in Bhutan. The Tak Sang cave monastery is another major pilgrimage site, perched precariously near the top of a 4,000-foot precipice. Within it is the sacred cave where Guru Padmasambhava is said to have meditated. Pilgrims also visit the cave hermitage at Tak-phu, which is still used for meditation retreats.

The monastic system is a principal branch of the Bhutanese government. It is headed by the *Je Kempo* who is elected by the Central Monastic Body and confirmed by the king. The stature of this office is on par with that of the king. Although the king authorizes financial support for the monasteries, he has no direct authority over them.[12]

The monastic tradition in Bhutan has served to preserve and protect Buddhism. Since Buddhism pervades Bhutanese culture so thoroughly, the monasteries' leadership in religious matters reaches into almost every home. The monks perform the ceremonies and rituals within each Buddhist family to mark the entire cycle of domestic events from birth to death. A family with a new house, for example, may invite a monk to bless the new home. At one such occasion, the author observed a fascinating annual ritual to bless the yaks for the coming year. A high lama presented offerings in an open air shrine and anointed the yaks between their festively decorated horns to insure their health and productivity. At the end of the ceremony, observers had to flee, as the yaks, blessed

but not particularly impressed, scampered out of the enclosure.

Buddhist festivals, with lamas performing the traditional religious dances, are important highlights of life in Bhutan (pages 30, 31). They not only reaffirm sacred beliefs, they are also occasions of community, beauty, and joy. *Tsechu* is a major festival held each autumn at the

Rotating a prayer wheel—a prevalent pastime among elderly men.

Four dancers performing the Dance of the Judgment of the Dead.

The monks also serve a significant role in the mundane affairs of everyday life. In Bhutan today, what we would regard as superstition abounds. Belief in demons, spirits, spells, and witchcraft is especially prevalent among the peasants. The anxieties and problems associated with bad weather, ill health, infertility, troubled relationships, and plain bad luck are often attributed to such forces, and the monks perform ancient rituals to help people counteract them.

Masked dancer showing the beautiful details of his costume.

Dancers vigorously exhibit their skills in this traditional dance.

various dzongs. Year after year, the ancient "Black Hat Dance" and the "Dance of the Judgment of the Dead" are performed here. Symbolizing themes such as placating evil spirits, the dances go on for three days, often culminating with the unfurling of a gigantic, appliqued thangka. One thangka of the Buddha is so large it covers the entire wall of a three-story temple (page 33). A high lama presides over the sacred rituals that accompany the festivals (page 32), and people from the surrounding areas arrive in their finest dress to watch intently, and to feast and play games (page 50).

The blowing of the traditional ceremonial conch at the festival—Wangdi Podrung.

Young monks kindle the incense in the braziers creating a special aura.

At the culmination of the annual festival at Wangdipodrung the high lama performs the traditional rites and makes offerings as the sound of the trumpets and conch shells fills the ancient courtyard.

Monks rush forward to gaze at the dazzling newly unfurled thangka, a mosaic of appliquéd symbols sacred to Lamaistic Buddhism. In the center is the image of Padmasambhava.

The Kempo of Gantey Gompa, in ceremonial dress, is the supervisor of instruction of the young monks.

A shaman at a festival practicing traditional medicine.

In ceremonial dress the governor or Dzonda of the Wangdipodrung District participates in the festival.

In an honored role, a young monk carries the ceremonial drums.

Four well dressed women wearing the finest kira cloth.

Procession of young lamas in the inner courtyard of Wangdipodrung.

At Tashicho temple square, Thimpu, monks soak up the sunlight before returning to their studies.

The Bhutanese monastic order is very hierarchical. At the bottom are the young monks, who are usually placed in the monastery at the age of five by their families who feel they are gaining merit and improving their karma by entering one son into the monastic life. For the little boys, however, this may be a transition filled with anxiety and fear. It has been observed that the young monks do adjust to the separation and regain their playfulness. Their initial depression is eventually replaced by a sense of brotherhood among their own age group (pages 38, 39).

Young monks do not receive the general public school education but are taught by the older monks a curriculum based on the Buddhist liturgy, involving the rote learning of texts used in ceremonies and rituals. Their discipline requires physical and mental stamina. At the age of fifteen, they are given the opportunity to leave the monastery, but in order to leave, they need their family's permission and enough money to reimburse the monastery for prior expenses. It is not common for monks to leave. Most choose to stay, and it is customary for them to remain for life.

Wash day for the young monks as they lay out their garments.

The young monks are pleased to be out of the damp Dzong and in the sun, following long hours of meditative chanting— Tongsa.

*A group of young monks relaxing at the Tashichho Dzong
following a long period of meditation.*

Bhutanese Arts and Crafts

BHUTANESE ART, like most Himalayan art, is an expression of religious devotion and is primarily used to enhance the teaching and practice of religion. Some of the traditional art forms are thangkas, mural-like wall paintings done in monasteries and lhakhangs, and the gigantic, highly revered, appliquéd thangkas that are unfurled only at annual festivals and special ceremonies. Woodcarving is another ancient tradition in Bhutan, where a school for woodcarvers was established in early times. Bhutan's forests yield a variety of hardwoods, especially sandalwood, that are well suited for carving the statuary and ornate pillars of the monasteries and temples. These sacred structures are also full of intricately carved cornices and struts that support the overhanging roofs.

There is little evidence of artistic achievement in Bhutan prior to the fifteenth century. The dominant cultural influences flowed into Bhutan from Tibet and, unlike the other Himalayan kingdoms, there was less direct artistic influence from India. Many pieces of religious art were brought into Bhutan by the migrating Tibetan Buddhist lamas during the fifteenth and sixteenth centuries. This artwork had been influenced by the Newari artists who came to Lhasa from Nepal in the preceding century. By the seventeenth century, with Tibetan culture firmly established in the valleys of Bhutan, Nepalese artists immi-

The forging of metal objects to become part of a shrine for the late King of Bhutan—Bumthang.

grated directly from Kathmandu. They built their own workshops and tutored Bhutanese apprentices in their techniques and styles of art. One of these workshops, specializing in silver and gold craftsmanship, still stands in Belnang.[13]

The production of art is a selfless act; aesthetic invention is not a goal. In Bhutan there is no "art for art's sake." Artists work to express their faith and to gain merit, not to achieve recognition from others. The work can be appreciated for its masterful representation of religious symbolism, fine detail, and excellent quality. Artistic excellence has not died out in this feudal kingdom. Religious art is state sponsored, and every year new architectural structures, murals, statues, and thangkas are created in the traditional way. Older works are refurbished periodically, especially the many fine mural paintings in the monasteries and lhakhangs, and artistic traditions continue with the king as patron (page 42).

Realizing the need to preserve the ancient techniques of painting and sculpture, the previous king established a training program for artists under the supervision of Bhutan's master painter. As part of their commitment to authenticity and tradition, painters follow the original formulas in making the mineral and vegetable dyes that provide their colors. Today Bhutan's Royal School of Art prepares a pool of young artists for service throughout the country. It is common to see teams of young artists working on sculptures, woodcarvings, and the interiors of sacred structures.

Artists and craftsmen continue to produce the typically Bhutanese, gigantic statues of the Buddha and Bodhisattvas, using age-old techniques. Fashioned out of clay that is hand-molded over wood and wire mesh frames, they are etched with fine details by teams of artists working on

Woman using a traditional belt loom.

A Statue of a Bodhisattva in preparation by a young local artist.

Details of Paro Dzong Bridge constructed in traditional manner.

scaffoldings, and then painted and gilded to give the appearance of being made of metal and stone. Eventually they are fitted with colorful brocade robes and banners and covered with jewelry. As in the past, artists are able to make these representations extremely evocative, whether they portray the sublimely blissful countenance of the Buddha or the wrathful deities that strike fear in the hearts of onlookers. A number of these large statues—some as high as twenty-five feet—will look down upon the practitioners in the new lhakhang being completed in Bumthang.

Large painted murals of enlightened beings or mandalas often decorate the portico walls of monasteries, temples, and lhakhangs. These often resemble thangkas and many are considered to be important works of art. Located in sacred places, they cannot fail to impress those who enter the shrines. The paintings that adorn the entrances of Paro and Wangdipodrung Dzongs are especially impressive. Both of these represent a unique mandala called the "Wheel of Life," or "Cycle of Existence," that illustrates the essential Buddhist belief about the stages of conditioned existence from birth through life, death, and rebirth. In symbolic form, it depicts the three "poisons"—passion, aggression, and ignorance—and the

Cosmic Mandala depicting the classical Buddhist cosmology—Paro Dzong.

six realms of existence they generate—the realms of the gods, humans, jealous gods, animals, hungry ghosts, and hell. The Wheel of Life teaches Buddhists about the interdependence of all phenomena, and the need to overcome the three poisons in order to be liberated from the "Wheel."

Bhutan is a visual feast. Everything is colorful—the varieties of flowers, the paintings on ordinary homes, the local costumes, the flying banners, and abundant hang-

Small chortens being laid out in front of a new Lhakhang built by the Queen Mother in memory of the late King in Bumthang.

There are many metal ornaments such as ceremonial bells, embossed sword handles, and ornate jewelry. There are exquisite baskets in everyday use, woven from fine bamboo strands dyed several different colors. Some of these crafts are sold through the Government Handicraft Emporium, but, by and large, this fine work is made for use at home and expresses the Bhutanese desire to have useful, beautiful objects.

Details of a well-constructed rural house near the Jakar Dzong.

Details of a cornice of a temple at Tashichho Dzong.

ings and offerings that adorn the shrines, temples, and monasteries. Moreover, intricately beautiful woodcarvings complete most structures, even the window frames of a common house. Whether this aesthetic environment is the result of religious inspiration or other cultural influences, the man-made environment of Bhutan is brilliant.

The tendency towards exuberance and high artistic standards spills over into the handicrafts of Bhutan.

Few countries can compete with Bhutan's handsome textiles, woven for local dress. Weaving is a cottage industry, and most homes have their own looms. Traditional back strap looms are used to weave the yarn into narrow cloth approximately twenty inches wide and sixty inches long. Several strips of this cloth are sewn together to make a *boku*, the male dress, or a *kira*, the women's national dress.[14] Except for a small number of people in

A portable shrine, called a tashigomang, exhibited at markets and festivals throughout the country.

A Tongsa farmer dressed in the typical Boku and straw hat.

the capital city, all Bhutanese wear traditional dress. The boku is a large garment, using up to four lengths of material. It is wrapped around a man's body and fastened with an ornate belt strap, allowing ample room for movement and storage. The kira is an elaborately embellished dress, drawn around the waist with a special belt and fastened at the neck with a pair of *koma*, or silver clasps. Bhutanese silk is often woven into the fabric used for women's garments, giving it an added brilliance (page 45).

Whatever the use, Bhutanese textiles are covered with geometric designs taken from nature or religious symbols. The natural motifs are obviously inspired by the environmental beauty that manifests everywhere in Bhutan. The religious symbols are centuries old, influenced by Bon as well as Buddhism. While there are significant regional differences in the use of color and design, the Bhutanese style of dress is quite similar from east to west. The people take great pride in their national dress, and even the poorest individuals can be seen at festivals wearing attractive costumes.

Over the centuries, art treasures have accumulated in the sacred monasteries of Bhutan. With few exceptions, these places of worship have always been open to the local people. No monetary value had ever been placed on works of art, but in recent times, as tourism has increased, many art objects have begun to vanish. It was discovered that foreigners were bribing local individuals to pilfer specific works of art from the shrines. One Bhutanese official discovered the crown of the second King of Bhutan, Jigme Wangchuk, in a Japanese museum. Now, in order to protect the national treasures, the King has limited outsiders' access to many holy places and visitors are more closely supervised. As in other Himalayan countries, there are tight customs controls upon leaving Bhutan.

Governance of Bhutan

BHUTAN'S PRESENT SYSTEM of government dates from the beginning of this century, when a monarchy was established. Today the monarch maintains strong central control, although certain elements of former governing systems still survive. In particular, the monastic orders continue to play a central role in the running of the country. The main components of Bhutan's government are the Office of the King, the National Assembly, the Royal Advisory Council, the Council of Ministers, the Central Monastic Body, the Judiciary, and various levels of local government.

The former King was deeply committed to reforming his government. Before his death in Africa, he had abolished serfdom and sought to bring about land reform. He had set up the Royal Advisory Council, the Council of Ministers, and the High Court; and he wisely separated the executive functions of government from the judiciary function. Furthermore, he had taken steps to reorganize the National Assembly. The National Assembly, or *Tshogdu*, advises the government on an array of important national matters, and develops and enacts legislation. It meets twice a year and on special occasions. It is made up of 150 members—one hundred chosen in the separate districts through consensus, ten elected by regional monastic bodies, and forty nominated by the king from other councils and departments. Any citizen twenty-five years or older is eligible to be elected. The Assembly allows open discussion on all matters. Voting is by secret ballot, with a simple majority required for passage of a law.

The Royal Advisory Council, or *Lodoi Tsokde*, advises the king and government ministers on all issues and oversees the policies and programs instituted by the Tshogdu. The Council is made up of ten members who represent the general population, including the largely Hindu southern Bhutanese, the monastics, and women. This council is always in session.

The Council of Ministers, the *Lyonpos*, is responsible for implementing the policies of such departments as Home Affairs, Education and Social Service, Commerce and Industry, Trade, Finance, Communications, Foreign Affairs, and Development. The ministers are appointed by the king and ratified by the Tshogdu.

The High Court, *Thimkang Gongma*, deals with civil and criminal matters and is separate from other branches of government. Judges are appointed by the King and are not required to be educated in jurisprudence. The civil and criminal code laid down by the seventeenth-century King Ngawang Namgyal is still, with some modifications, the law of the land and represents his humane spirit and values. Although this court is all powerful, the king is still the highest "court" of appeal. He is available to all his subjects, and it is well known that he may be approached personally and petitioned on matters large or small as he walks to his office.

Bhutan is divided into seventeen regional districts. The

traditional dzongs continue to be the centers of administrative and political activity. They do not, however, have the power they had under the previous system and are supervised by the staff of the Central Civil Service. The district officers, *Dzongdas*, are responsible to the Home Minister. The judge of the district court, the *Thrimpon*, is the regional magistrate.

On the local level, the smaller administrative units of the villages enjoy a greater degree of autonomy. The headmen, called *Gaps*, or *Mandals*, are elected for three-year terms. They have a great deal of freedom to find solutions to local problems without interference from higher authorities.

Sounding through each level of government is the voice of the monastic orders, headed by the *Je Khempo*, who presides over all the monastic institutions in the country. This position is nominated by the Central Monastic Body, with the King's consent.

At the apex of this many-tiered system is the King. His voice, if considerate and reasonable, is the dominant one. His values and policies have a profound effect on his people. Because of the King's approach to development, Bhutan is making significant strides towards modernization while avoiding the destructive forces which affect most other developing nations. The present King cherishes Bhutanese culture and feels that it is his mission to protect it from the onslaught of ideas, values, or materials which might destroy it. As a result, Bhutan is successfully entering the twenty-first century with its windows and doors opened just narrowly to the outside, avoiding much of the cultural disruption of Nepal and Ladakh. It is true that the King is paternalistic towards his people, but it is also true that the people have profound reverence for him and his policies.

Bhutan recently completed its fifth five-year economic plan. With strong financial backing from India, it has developed the roads, power, and communications systems necessary for the country to survive in the modern world.

Until now, ninety percent of the Bhutanese people have lived by farming and raising livestock. New economic development has focused on plans for the wise use of natural resources, such as the extensive forests and untapped mineral reserves. There is great potential for growth in these industries, but they must be developed in ways which preserve the lifestyles of the people and the natural economy. To date, these resources have barely been tapped. Technical competence is still generally lacking in many fields; and with the shortage of labor, more guest workers would be needed to fill many positions.[15]

Only a few small industries have been developed so far. For instance, in Bumthang there is a cannery that bottles apple juice, a cheese factory, and a metal woodstove factory. Some farmers are being encouraged to pursue single cash-crop farming. In the east, vast acreages of potatoes are being grown for export to India. It remains to be seen how formerly subsistent farmers will fare growing food for export, rather than just for their own table.

Since 1960, well over 150 primary and secondary schools have been built. Many of these are boarding schools. The government policy is to put a mix of children from different parts of the country into each school to encourage cross-cultural sharing and to strengthen the national identity.

Bhutan's most significant world partner is India. Following the departure of the British, a treaty was signed with India ensuring that she be consulted regarding all of Bhutan's foreign agreements. India, in turn, is obliged to help protect Bhutan's borders. In 1959, for instance, after the Chinese took over Tibet, the Indian Army had to show force along Bhutan's eastern frontier to forestall an invasion. In addition, India provides Bhutan with the rupees necessary to run its government.

There continues to be a problem providing enough qualified staff to run the Bhutanese government and national projects. Formerly, the practice was to educate members of the royal family or bright young boys from the villages to fill these various roles. Later, personnel was borrowed from India to staff important technical positions. Now these positions are being filled by Bhutanese who have obtained higher education in India and, more recently, in western countries.[16]

Bhutan is an active member of a number of international organizations such as the United Nations, UNESCO, UNICEF, the World Bank, and the World Health Organization. As a non-aligned country, it is a member of the Colombo Plan. Through these organizations, Bhutan receives consultants and other assistance in many areas related to development.

Part Two
NEPAL

*Although far from the capitol of Kathmandu, the father in
this family is dressed in the formal Nepali style—
near Mt. Kangenchunga.*

*Mt. Annapurna, in west central Nepal, the first peak
over 24,000 feet to be climbed.*

The morning mist hangs low in the valley leading to Mt. Makalu (26,500 feet).

The Land

Nepal, by far the largest of the three kingdoms, is a landlocked country with an area of 55,463 square miles, lying between 26° to 30° north latitude and 80° to 88° longitude. Basically rectangular in shape, it is approximately 500 miles long and 150 miles wide. Resting along its northern and eastern boundaries are the four highest peaks in the world: Mount Sagamartha, or Everest, at 29,795 feet; Mount Kangchenjunga, 28,289 feet; Mount Makalu, 27,807 feet; and Mount Dhaulagiri, 26,795 feet. India borders Nepal on the south, east, and west. Tibet is to the north.

The physical geography of all three kingdoms has strongly influenced their history, culture, and economic life. Nepal has been shaped by its rugged landscape, diverse ecological niches, and its two giant neighbors.[17] Nepal's physical characteristics can best be described by the varying altitudes. The country can be divided into four main zones stacked from south to north: the lower plains, the inner valley basins, the sub-Himalayan region, and the Himalayan region.

The low-lying terrain, or Tarai, is a continuation of the plains of northern India. A narrow, torrid strip of land, lying 200 to 1,000 feet above sea level, the Tarai was mostly an impenetrable jungle until the 1970s, when much of it was cleared for farmland. Enriched by the annual monsoon rains and alluvial floods, its sandy soil is suitable for intensive agriculture. This region is now considered the rice bowl of Nepal.

A gigantic mani stone on the path leading to Tangboche Monastery and Mt. Everest.

The major road in Nepal runs from east to west through the Tarai. The tropical rain forests along the northern border of the region still abound with tigers, elephants, rhinoceros, bears, buffalo, and a myriad of exotic birds. At the Royal Chitawan National Park, a government game reserve, one can ride elephants through the high grass to observe these animals in their natural habitat. Yet, the deforestation of the rain forests is a constant threat, and their protection is an ongoing concern.

The Valley Basin Zone lies between the Himalayas and the Mahabhrat and Siwalik Hills. The basins include Kathmandu Valley, Pokara Basin, the Salyantar, Karputar, Rumjatar, and Tumlingtar valleys, and some smaller basins. They have been formed either by river deposits or the drying up of lakes. Sitting at elevations of 4,000 to 10,000 feet, the many basins have vastly different climates and vegetation, yielding a great variety of produce for the market (page 56).

Kathmandu Valley, at 4,500 feet, is the largest of the basins. A richly fertile area, it is farmed intensively, as are the surrounding hills, which are heavily terraced and ascend like steps into the heavens. With its fertile soil, agreeable climate, and central location on the crossroads of Tibet and India, the Kathmandu Valley has been a center of high civilization for more than a thousand years.

The Sub-Himalayan Region extends from 6,000 to 16,000 feet along the length of Nepal. Tectonic forces have disrupted the mountains here, creating many deep chasms. Rivers originating in the Himalayas flow southward through these chasms onto the Tarai and, finally, the plains of India. Along the way, they have deposited small areas of flat land which are marginally suitable for agriculture and human habitation. Some of these areas are densely overpopulated, forcing the farmers to use the higher slopes. Their terraces sometimes climb as far as the eye can see.

Planting crops and cutting wood for fuel has had a devastating effect on these slopes. Every year, the heavy monsoon rains and hailstorms cause devastating landslides. After years of backbreaking toil, farmers may find whole areas of their terraced farms swept away. At times, entire villages disappear in the landslides. Flying above or walking through these hills, one sees the heavy scarring of the land. Life is difficult here, as men and women struggle with the environment.

The Himalayan Region at 16,000 to 29,000 feet above sea level, is often called the "roof of the world." Here Mount Sagamartha, or Everest, the name given to it by Westerners, reigns supreme over the fourteen other Nepalese mountains that soar to over 25,000 feet. The perpetual snow line starts at about 17,500 feet, and broad rushing torrents originate from the many glacier systems in this region. Raging rivers from the valleys of the inner Himalayas in Tibet also drain through this area. Although the mountains of Tibet to the north are lower, their deep gorges slice through this massive mountain range. The gorge that forms the Arun River starts at about 24,000 feet and drops to 2,000 feet in the Tarai, making it the deepest valley in the world.[18]

Nepal is perhaps best known to the outside world for its great mountains and climbers who have attempted to ascend them. Since 1959, when Sir Edmund Hilary and Norgay Tinzing first climbed the peak of Mount Sagamartha, a steady stream of climbers have come to scale her peaks. Lying on the border between Nepal and Tibet, Sagamartha was climbed in May of 1988 by two teams of climbers who met at the top after starting out simultaneously from the Tibetan and Nepali sides. Mountain

Standing on the middle range of mountains at 8,000 feet one can see rice terraces ascending to the sky and descending to the lower valleys.

Autumn harvest of rice being thrashed and winnowed—near Pokara.

climbing and trekking are the major attractions in Nepal, bringing in sportsmen, tourists, and foreign cash.

With continuous natural disasters—earthquakes, monsoons, hailstorms, and the effects of raging rivers—Nepal is constantly in a state of disequilibrium. Social planners worry about the long-term effects of overcrowding and land degradation. Overpopulation and a rising birthrate are recent phenomena. But the washing away of topsoil is an age-old problem that does not promise to go away. The fertile plains of India would not exist without the annual drama of flooding rivers that carry off the fertile Nepalese soil. The only solution to the problems of land, food, and fuel shortages is population control. There is a clear equation between overpopulation, deforestation, and land degradation. These problems have drawn international attention, and foreign aid programs have launched family planning and reforestation efforts.[19]

The destruction of the Tangboche Monastery in 1989 by fire provides an example of the caution which must be taken around well-meaning efforts to bring positive

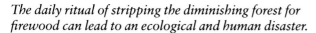

The daily ritual of stripping the diminishing forest for firewood can lead to an ecological and human disaster.

Suspension bridges, such as this one in the Manang area, can save hours or sometimes days of walking for Nepalese porters.

A well cared for Yak standing near Tangboche Monastery.

change to developing countries such as Nepal. It was in this year that electricity was brought, by the means of small generators, to this isolated Buddhist monastery at the foot of Mount Sagamartha. For the first time the monks had affordable energy to use for heating. Not understanding the hazard, a monk standing near an electric heater had his robe ignited, and the resulting fire destroyed this magnificent monastery.

People of Nepal

A COMPREHENSIVE SURVEY OF the peoples and cultures of Nepal would require several volumes. The country has more than forty ethnic groups and thirty-six discrete languages.[20] Until recently, there was no accurate accounting of this great diversity of the Nepalese people. Only since the 1950s has Nepal been open to outsiders. Traveling within Nepal was always on foot—human or animal. Separated by the rugged terrain, the many peoples and cultures within Nepal's borders were unknown even to the Nepalese themselves (pages 60–63, 64, 65).

In the 1960s, Professor Dor Bahadur Bista, a Nepali anthropologist, undertook a field survey of the various ethnic groups and their characteristics. In the first edition of his book, *Peoples of Nepal*, Dr. Bista used geographic classifications—Middle Hills and Valley People, Terai People, Himalayan People—to describe the mosaic of Nepalese groups.[21] In subsequent editions, however, he has rejected this classification system, describing instead dynamic patterns of ethnic groups moving through time and place. The groups are in flux, flowing from north to south, from west to east, and from rural to urban areas. Over time, as they move, traditional barriers are breaking down, and the diverse and geographically separated Nepalese tribes are evolving into an integrated, culturally mixed society. This is a slow process—integrating race, religion, ethnicity, caste, and class—with the real blending occurring first in the Nepalese cities (pages 61, 64, 65).[22]

A young Gurung girl, with Machhupuchhare in the background, rests on the way to collect grain—near Ghandrung.

A peasant girl from the Gurung ethnic group.

In order to understand the current divergent population, we need to look at the migrations and historical events that shaped it. The original inhabitants of Nepal were *Dravidians*, related to the early settlers of southern India. Little trace of them remains. The first people to colonize Nepal were probably Mongols from the north who settled in the highest valleys of the Himalayas. They were followed by Aryan groups from India, who settled at lower elevations. The Aryans·were the descendents of western hordes who settled in northern India centuries before the Christian era. They had Mediterranean facial features and physiques. The earliest group of Aryans to reach Nepal were probably the *Chetris*, who spoke a language akin to present-day Nepali. Settling in the hilly area, the Chetris are the largest Nepalese group today.

The Hindu Brahmins, a priestly caste, also came north from India and settled in the hills, where they strongly imposed their religion and caste system on local inhabi-

Local dress changes from valley to valley, and hill to hill. Here a farmer from eastern Nepal with his local garb and adornments.

Jewelry worn by women often represents the accummulated family wealth.

A woman at the Chainpur market.

An elderly gentleman returning home with sheaths of rice.

A main thoroughfare leading through this village in the Manang area.

tants. Leather workers, for instance, were regarded as "untouchables." The age-old occupational, dietary, marital, and social customs are still practiced.

Successive waves of migration came from the south, struggling through the malaria-infested jungles of the Tarai into Nepal. Many of the immigrant groups were escaping the ravages of the Moghul invaders of India. From the north came migrations of Tibetans in search of fertile land. The *Gurungs*, *Magars*, *Kratis-Rais* and *Tamangs* were some of the larger Tibetan groups to settle in the middle hills as farmers. These are peoples with Mongoloid features, and they speak a Tibeto-Burmese tongue.[23]

Also from Tibet came the *Sherpas*, best known today for their mountaineering skill and heroism. From the time of the British Raj on the subcontinent, Sherpa tribesmen have helped mountaineers scale the highest peaks of Nepal. This small tribe has made an important contribution to Nepal and is a major human resource for its tourist industry. Their main community is at Namche Bazaar in the Solo Khumbu region; they are also scattered throughout the mountainous areas to the west.

The *Newars* are another small but culturally significant group. They speak a Tibeto-Burmese dialect and are a combination of Mongol and Aryan racial groups. Evolving over 2,500 years in the fertile Kathmandu Valley, their ancient civilization was the essence of what was then Nepal. The Newars, whose culture still dominates the Kathmandu Valley, are city dwellers with a long tradition of trade, arts and crafts, architecture, and literature. Their culture is complex and rich, with its own music, rituals, and festivals. They practice both Hinduism and Buddhism, and freely weave aspects of both into their religious lives.

Until the eighteenth century, the Kathmandu Valley was not unlike Tuscany during the Italian Renaissance. At the height of the Newar civilization, there were several city-states, each with its own patron prince, competing for supremacy, power, and prestige. Cities such as Patan, Bhaktapur (Bhadgaon), and Kathmandu were centers of this high culture. The extraordinary Newar architecture

This well-dressed Newari woman stands at the portico of her finely crafted house entrance.

and fine wood and metal craftsmanship still exist today; the complex Newari cultural celebrations still mark the annual calendar. As increasing numbers of Newari traders migrated throughout the kingdom to become merchants and shop owners in the village bazaars, their unique culture, architecture, and crafts have spread to many districts (page 65).

Further south in the Tarai are the *Tharus* and *Danuwars*, tribal peoples with Mongoloid features. They are the very early, if not indigenous, inhabitants of this area. Living in small villages, they till the land, fish, and hunt. More recently, new groups of Chetris and Brahmins have arrived in the Tarai from the plains of India. These immigrants still maintain close ties with their roots in India, as they practice a more orthodox type of Hinduism and are engaged mainly in farming and commerce.

The Tarai, formerly a malaria-infested swampy jungle, is now being cleared for settlement. Pressured by the need

While poor, Nepalese take pride in the quality of their construction. This house appears with Mt. Annapurna in the background.

A major source of income in this region comes from the retirement pay of ex-Gurka soldiers such as this—Ghandrung, with Mt. Annapurna in the background.

for more land, families of various ethnic backgrounds are moving to this flat, fertile farmland, and the Tarai forests are quickly disappearing. National authorities recognize that there is a limit to the numbers of people the Tarai can absorb.

The most recent migration into Nepal started in the 1950s with the Chinese invasion of Tibet. When the fourteenth Dalai Lama fled his country in 1959, large numbers of Tibetans followed him on foot over Himalayan passes. Many refugees from the upper strata of Tibetan society settled in the Kathmandu and Pokara valleys, and their culture is being infused into the already rich blend of Nepalese society. Many other Tibetans are still isolated in refugee camps, under difficult living conditions, waiting to be resettled.

It is remarkable how such a variety of remote ethnic groups, with its vast variety of languages, have come together as a nation. Until the last half of the eighteenth century, Nepal was a collection of competitive, warring mini-kingdoms stretched across the southern slopes of the Himalayas. Although the Newars of Kathmandu Valley enjoyed an advanced civilization, the remainder of the country was backward by contemporary standards. The thrust for unification was spearheaded by King Prithvi Narayan Shah, from Gorkha, a small kingdom in the west. He declared *Nepali* the national language and ordered it taught throughout Nepal. Today more than half the Nepalese speak Nepali along with their mother tongue. With a common language, an expanding highway system, and several small airports, Nepal is experiencing an increased sense of national identity. The physical and social barriers that separate groups are breaking down. Yet the search for new farmland goes on, with the population moving higher into the hills and onto the newly cleared land in the Tarai.

A Tibetan trader, a not unfamiliar sight on the Jomson trail.

In from a hard day's work carrying loads, a group of porters rest at the bazaar hoping to find something they can afford with the few rupees they make.

A caravan comes down the ancient Jomson trail from Mustang or perhaps Tibet loaded with trade items.

History of Nepal

THE HISTORICAL EVENTS THAT turned this 500-mile stretch of rugged mountain valleys and diverse peoples into a unified kingdom is fascinating, bloodcurdling, and complex. Consider the bold lust for land that motivated Nepal to invade and subdue powerful Tibet with its allied Chinese-Mongol army, and to do battle with the warriorlike Sikhs in Kashmir. Prior to this thrust toward nationhood in the nineteenth century, there was no political entity known as Nepal, just a series of tribal states, similar to Europe in the Middle Ages.

According to legend, the Buddhist sage Manjusri came to Nepal from China, and, in a large lake, he saw a vision of Lord Buddha in the shape of a lotus blossom. After meditating for a while, the sage struck the edge of the lake a hefty blow with his sword, and a river began to flow from it, miraculously draining the lake and revealing the Kathmandu Valley.

The first inhabitants of the valley were the *Gopals* and *Ahirs*, cow-herders and buffalo-keepers. Later the *Kirats* created the first dynasty there, but little else is known about them. In the second century, the *Lichichavi Kingdom* took root in the valley, and flourished until the end of the ninth century. This high civilization created finely sculptured shrines that still exist today, dedicated to their Hindu and Buddhist deities.

In the seventh century, the Lichichavi King Amshu-varma gave his daughter Bhrikuti, a devout Buddhist, to the Tibetan King Srong-San-Gampo (629–650) in marriage. The Tibetan King had one other wife, a Chinese Buddhist princess, and together she and Bhrikuti are credited with establishing Buddhism throughout Nepal and Tibet. King Srong-San-Gampo also established the first Buddhist monasteries in Bhutan. During this period, Kathmandu was already carrying on official relations with China, Tibet, and India.

Little is known about the history of Nepal for the three centuries following the Lichichavi Dynasty, which ended around the year 879, until the thirteenth century, when two powerful dynasties emerged. First there was a new stirring in western Nepal. As a result of the Muslim invasions of India, the *Rajputs* were pushed north from Rajistan into the Tarai and then into the hills around the Kali Gandaki and Mahakali rivers. The Rajputs created the powerful *Chaubisi Kingdoms*, which lasted for several centuries. The kingdoms became smaller and weaker over time, due to the traditional practice of a king dividing up his land among his sons, until this area was divided into forty-six separate kingdoms, each with its own ruler.

Meanwhile, still in the thirteenth century, the Malla Dynasty was coming to power in the Kathmandu Valley. Ari Malla conquered the entire valley, consolidated it into a kingdom, and assumed the throne. This was the beginning of a highly influential dynasty that ruled for five centuries, until it was conquered by the Gorkhas from the west. As the richest land in that part of Asia, the Valley was subject to constant invasion. Armies from the western Malla Kingdom—no relation to the one in Kathmandu—unsuccessfully invaded the valley three times between 1288 and 1313. Then in 1350, a Muslim Shah of the Bengal army invaded with his troops, and devastated many Hindu and Buddhist temples, shrines, and sacred monuments, as Muslims had done throughout India and southeast Asia.

The Malla Dynasty developed one of the most advanced civilizations in Asia during this millennium. Although confined to a small geographic area, its impact reached into Tibet, India, and China. By the end of the fourteenth century, Jayasthiti Malla had created a tightly structured, well-administered society. Within a classical feudal system of government, land was distributed among his loyal nobles, and a rigidly defined caste system was set up and strictly enforced. Although not benign, it provided a structure for community life in this urban society.

Before Jayasthiti's grandson Yakshya Malla (ca. 1428 to 1500) died, he divided the kingdom among his three sons, creating the three separate city-states of Kathmandu, Patan, and Bhaktapur. Although this move weakened the power of the dynasty, it stimulated an environment of great artistic achievement.

The sons and their descendents fought among themselves. Conflict eventually arose over control of the trade routes to Tibet, the lifelines to the small, mercantile city-states. Bhaktapur's control of the passes leading into Tibet was forcibly wrested away by Kathmandu, which then contracted to mint coins for Tibet. These events increased Kathmandu's trade with Tibet, leaving Bhaktapur and Patan in a weakened financial position.

These conflicts continued for several hundred years, while each of the city-states continued to develop its own culture and arts to an even higher degree. Monuments to their gods and rulers proliferated. The rulers supported the arts, and the principalities became places of singular beauty. Their squabbling, however, distracted them from

guarding the valley from attack. This was a very real and demanding task, since the ring of steep hills surrounding the valley was difficult to defend.

Events were developing to the west which would eventually topple the weakened defenses of the rival states of Kathmandu Valley. One of the major Rajput families, the *Shahs*, fled to Nepal after being defeated by powerful Moghul invaders, and they settled in the Gandaki region in eastern Nepal. The Shahs were a powerful military family, originally from Udaipur. Within a hundred years after fleeing the Moghuls, they had managed to take over a large area of western Nepal and establish a kingdom there. (The current King of Nepal is a direct descendent of this family.) In 1559, Prince Dravya Shah moved eastward, settling in Gorkha, a province about fifty miles west of Kathmandu. A man of considerable ability, the prince became involved in a coup and became the ruler of Gorkha. Once in control, he and his successors continued to expand their territory.

Almost two centuries later, in 1742, his descendent Prithvi Narayan Shah succeeded to the Gorkha throne. Shah was acutely aware of Kathmandu Valley's weak defenses, and of the city-states' inability to unite. With an eye on Kathmandu, his army fought its way eastward, occupying first the Nuwakot Valley and then capturing the strategic passes to Tibet. The critical trade routes from Kathmandu to Tibet were severed. A resistance was organized by the Malla ruler of Kathmandu, but the Gorkha army of Prithvi Narayan Shah continued bit by bit to encircle the valley. Capturing all the strategic hill points, Shah's army sealed off all of the trade routes in and out of the valley, and the three city-states were isolated.

One by one, the small towns in the valley were invaded and captured. Patan, next to Kathmandu, surrendered when it found itself thoroughly isolated, and Prithvi Shah ascended its throne. Next, King Jaya Prakash Malla of Kathmandu capitulated, although not without fighting, along with the allied British Army, to resist the invasion. The British forces were ambushed, however, and suffered heavy losses. When Prithvi Shah entered Kathmandu city, the people were celebrating an annual festival. The great throne stood empty, awaiting the arrival of the Malla king—whereupon Prithvi Shah entered the scene and took the seat himself.

The Kings of Patan and Kathmandu fled to Bhaktapur, which refused to surrender but was soon occupied without much difficulty. Thus ended twenty-six years of conquest. In 1769 all of the Kathmandu Valley was under the control of Prithvi Shah and his Gorkha army, and the Malla Dynasty had ended.

Not content with his conquest of the valley, Prithvi Shah continued to expand his kingdom. As his army marched eastward battling small kingdoms and tribal villages, valley after valley fell. Using firearms against the Nepali's primitive bows and arrows, his army overcame all resistance. When Prithvi Shah died in 1775, his kingdom extended to the present border of Sikkim.

His successor died after a brief, three-year rule, but his successor's widow and regent, Rajendra Lakshmi, a woman of strong determination and leadership, took control of the country and continued the consolidation of Nepal. Under her leadership, the military conquered the western kingdom of Lamjung. Following her death, an uncle of the minor King, Bahadur Shah, became the regent and continued his predecessors' expansionist march to the west. Behind this record of continuous conquest was a grandiose dream of a Himalayan state composed of all tribal groups across the southern Himalayas. Soon the conquered territories lay far beyond the existing borders of Nepal, in Kashmir to the west and Sikkim in the east.

Prithvi Shah and his immediate successors had maintained good relations with Tibet. Now, however, Nepal was growing so powerful and aggressive that the expansion of its boundaries vexed Tibet. When the Tibetan ruler frustrated Bahadur Shah's efforts to keep open communication channels with China, Bahadur Shah's army invaded southern Tibet, going as far as Xigatse. The army returned to Nepal with sacred religious booty from a leading monastery and high-ranking military leaders as prisoners.

At this time China, because of its strategic importance, had more than a maternal interest in the affairs of Tibet and was challenging its sovereignty. When word of the Nepalese invasion got to the Manchu Emperor of China, he sent his troops into Tibet to expel them. But the Chinese military forces, although superior in numbers to the Nepalese, were unaccustomed to the high-altitude terrain. They became bogged down in the rugged passes as they pursued the Nepalese south across the Himalayas. The two forces finally reached a standoff, and a treaty was signed.

Nepal continued its expansionist policies, moving its armies westward until they encroached upon the Sikhs, interfering with their intentions in the Punjab. The Sikhs, another warrior tribe, were a superior force physically and militarily. They successfully pushed the Nepalese back to their western boundary.

Meanwhile in the Tarai to the south, Nepal, like Bhutan, was engaged in a war with British India. Each claimed ownership of this fertile region. The Nepalese excelled over the British in combat, inflicting heavy losses. In the long run, however, they had to capitulate to the much larger, better-equipped British army. In doing so, Nepal lost many of the districts it had conquered. In 1816 it signed a treaty with the British that firmly fixed the southern boundaries. An official British Resident was set up in Kathmandu. According to the treaty, Nepal's foreign policy would now be dictated by the British foreign office, Whitehall in London. This period marked the beginning of enforced isolation from the outside world.

The ruling Shah family began to lose its power. Two kings in succession came to the throne too young to rule. Consequently the country was governed by a series of prime ministers. The first one, Bhimsen Thapa (1806–1835), was an able administrator. In 1846, the powerful *Rana* family came to rule, with Jung Bahadur serving as their first prime minister. The Ranas ruled Nepal for seven generations until 1950. The Shah kings kept up the show of royalty, but were political puppets. Jung Bahadur was ruthless and autocratic, and filled all official positions with his relatives. His successors were also notoriously self-serving. The Nepalese people were kept in poverty and ignorance, except for the small upper class that supported the regime. Contacts with the outside world were kept to a minimum, and even the social progress in India surpassed development in Nepal.

The Rana family rulers maintained a good relationship with the British who, under Queen Victoria, accepted if not condoned the Ranas' despotic rule. The most progressive of the Ranas, Chandra Shumshere, ruled during the first quarter of this century. He abolished slavery and managed to revoke the 1816 Treaty with Britain. The new treaty recognized Nepal as a sovereign land, able to determine its own foreign policy and establish diplomatic relations abroad.

Upon gaining independence in 1947, India provided an unexpected counterpoint in this region. A newly formed democratic state now bordered a feudal kingdom. King Tribhuvan of Nepal took advantage of this situation to try to reinstate the power of the Shah monarchy and end the Ranas' tyrannical rule. India pressured Rana leaders to reform their government, but they resisted. Realizing the possibility of support from India, King Tribhuvan seized the moment and, in a public gesture against the Rana tyranny, took refuge in the Indian Embassy. Popular support quickly gathered for the ouster of the Ranas and the return of the monarchy. In a 1951 revolution, the Ranas were routed, and the leadership of the Kingdom was restored to the Shah family. Nepal now opened its borders to the outside world. King Tribhuvan's goal was to move the state towards a representative government. However, his rule lasted only four years, until 1955, when his son, King Mahendra, assumed power.

Since the time of King Mahendra, Nepal has become open to the modern world, although in many places daily life is still basically at the level of a feudal society. By the international standards applied to developing countries, Nepal is still backward. In spite of considerable money and consultation aimed at improving living conditions, more needs to be done.

Over the centuries Nepal, as is true in the case of Bhutan, has been playing a balancing act between its overpowering neighbors. Following the establishment of the modern state of Nepal in 1951, both China and India have continued to seek influence in Nepal's state of internal affairs. While attempting to play the game to its advantage through accepting loans and aid, Nepal has sacrificed some of its autonomy. For example, in 1988 it had to temper its humanitarian largess towards Tibetan refugees fleeing from the suppression in Lhasa by forcibly

High in the mountains this teacher and his students wait anxiously for the UNESCO educational supplies to come, so they that can study.

handing over a number of them to their Chinese persecutors at the border.

Trouble with its southern neighbor erupted again in 1989. Nepal found that all of its borders with India, except two, were closed to international traffic. In sealing the borders, India cut off supplies of essential foods, medicines, and fuels, creating a severe shortage and spiraling inflation. Furthermore, this resulted in Nepal having to revert to harvesting more of its diminishing forest to provide the needed fuel.

The action of India in failing to renew well established bilateral trade and transit agreements was caused in part by Nepal's acceptance of military equipment and supplies from China. Nepal's vulnerability as a small, landlocked country bordered by these two powerful neighbors, often adversaries, requires a non-aligned policy. Yet, it still needs to react strategically to events often beyond its control.

Nepal's continuous need to accept aid and technical assistance from its neighbors will carry with it the requirement to repay the largess by bending to unacceptable policies and compromising or weakening its sovereignty.

Religion in Nepal

HINDUISM IS THE STATE religion of Nepal. The King and his family are staunch followers of that faith, as are most Nepalese people. Nevertheless Nepal has the greatest diversity of religions of the three kingdoms, and there are both Buddhist and Bon-po practitioners here, as well as a large number of Muslims in the Tarai. What is unique to Nepal is its eclectic approach to religion (page 73).

As in Bhutan, the indigenous Bon religion is still practiced in the more remote tribes and among the *Dolpo*, *Thakali*, and *Baragunule* people. Some of the Bon rituals have been incorporated into Buddhism, as well, with some differences: the circumambulation of chortens and the twirling of prayer wheels, for example, are done counterclockwise. Buddhism is more common among the people living in higher mountainous regions. Tribal groups such as the *Tamangs*, *Sunwars*, and the *Rai* are Buddhist; still it is not uncommon for some of these tribes to include Hindu rituals in their ceremonies (page 73).

Until the sixth century, Buddhism was the principal religion in Nepal. The practice then was closer to the basic teachings of the Buddha than the vajrayana, or tantric, Buddhism practiced there today. The two great *stupas*, Bodhnath and Swayambhunath, in Kathmandu Valley were Buddhist pilgrimage sites as early as the second century B.C.E.

The *Sherpas*, who are of Tibetan origin, are the best-known Buddhist group in Nepal. Practitioners of the

The magnificence of Bhaktapur can be appreciated as viewed from the steps of a temple.

A weathered row of mani stores stretches toward Mt. Ama Dablan near Tangboche Monastery.

On a long pilgrimage to the Great Stupa at Swayambunath, this young peasant from the Dolpo region signs on as a porter for a trekking group.

Local Hindu shrines appear on almost every street in Kathmandu.

The shrine of Pushupatinath on the Bagmati River serves as a cremation site for both Hindus and Buddhists.

The reading of palms to foretell the future.

Nyingma School of Tibetan Buddhism, the Sherpas share common religious interests with the Tibetan Buddhists even today. In the Solu-Kumbu region, a major Sherpa center in the east, the landscape is dotted with Buddhist reminders. At the Tangboche, in the shadows of Mount Sagamartha, there is a magnificent monastery, headquarters of the monastic body. Here at 12,000 feet above sea level, the annual week-long *Mani Rimdu* festival is held in the open air, with monks performing ceremonies and masked dances for an enthusiastic audience of villagers.

But in the Kathmandu Valley, the Hindu gods reign supreme. Town and village centers are dominated by elab-

A common greeting among the Buddhists and Hindus is this sacred salutation.

A Hindu mendicant priest, or Sadhu, communicates his message through both word and gesture.

In Nepal a temple is more than a place of worship—here it is serving as a place for peaceful repose for a mother and child in from the fields—Kirtipur, Kathmandu Valley.

orate temples and pagodas adorned with mythological creatures and skillfully carved representations of the vast pantheon of Hindu gods. The pillars and beams of these temples are embellished with beautifully carved scenes, and most homes have small shrines decked with fresh offerings to their patron deities. The prevailing imagery is taken from Hindu tantric iconography.

Two forms of Hinduism are practiced in the Kathmandu region: Hindu Tantra, long established there and generally followed by the masses; and a more orthodox form introduced by the Brahmans who fled from the Muslims to Nepal. This form, with its traditional caste system, was later reinforced when the Hindu Gorkha rul-

A lama and his retinue en route to the monastary by Mt. Tamserku.

Approaching the top of the mount where Swayambunath is located, one passes a row of meditating Buddhas.

This Buddhist monk serves as a guardian at the Great Stupa of Swayambunath.

ers established their kingdom in Kathmandu Valley in the eighteenth century.

Hindu festivals are pivotal to the life of the community. There is a celebration for almost every day of the year. The *Durga Puja* is the most important, lasting for ten days to commemorate the victory of the Goddess Durga over a demon in the form of a buffalo. During this holiday scores of buffalo and goats are sacrificed to the goddess. The symbolism of the festival brings together the beliefs of both popular forms of Hinduism. *Diwali* is another important Hindu holiday observed throughout the kingdom.

Two outstanding Buddhist monuments stand in the Kathmandu Valley, the great stupas of Swayambhunath and Bodhnath. The former, on a hill overlooking the city, is alleged to be over 2,500 years old, the oldest Buddhist holy place in Nepal. The all-seeing eyes of Buddha are depicted on the four sides of a great cube resting on a huge white dome. The Bodhnath Stupa a few miles away is nearly as old and is one of the largest stupas in Asia. Today it is encircled by a Tibetan refugee camp. Both stupas play a large part in the religious life of the community.

The ancient Pashupatinath temple, a few miles from the center of Kathmandu, is the most holy Hindu shrine in Nepal, attracting pilgrims from all over India. It is dedicated to Shiva, a five-headed deity. In the inner part of the temple stands the sacred *lingam*, the symbol of the male organ. Only the highest Brahmin priests are allowed inside the temple. Pashupatinath is built on the banks of the sacred Baghmati River, similar to Varanasi (Benares) on the banks of the Ganges. Nearby are shelters where the terminally ill await death. Pious Hindus believe their salvation is assured if they are cremated on the banks of the Baghmati river (page 40).

This man is making merit as he circumambulates the stupa twirling each of the hundreds of prayer wheels.

Nepalese Arts and Crafts

Nepalese have little need to import cookware. This shop specializes in the sale of brass pots and cauldrons.

THROUGHOUT RECORDED HISTORY, Nepal has made a significant contribution to Himalayan art. After perfecting their own techniques of architecture, stone and metal sculpture, and painting, Nepalese artists and craftsmen extended their artistic influence into Tibet, China, and Japan.[24] The unique civilization of Kathmandu Valley provided a fertile atmosphere for artistic development. It is believed that the pagoda, the graceful multi-storied temple, was first designed in Nepal and spread from here into China and Japan. Chinese traders described seeing this innovation in Nepal as early as the seventh century.

The main themes of Nepal's art have always been Buddhist and Hindu. From the sixth to the ninth centuries, during the Lichichavi Civilization, Nepalese artists displayed outstanding creative abilities; and from the thirteenth to the fifteenth centuries, artistic achievement reached its peak. The famous Nepalese artist, Arniko (1245–1306), along with eighty other artists, moved to Lhasa in Tibet, where the Nepalese made a lasting impression on Tibetan art. Arniko also traveled to Beijing where he was commissioned to work for Kublai Khan.[25]

Today the Kathmandu Valley is a vast open-air museum with fine examples of art—temples ornamented with stone figures or beautifully rendered metal fountains—created over a span of a thousand years. The ancient name, "Kathmandu Valley," literally means the "Valley of Wooden Temples," temples which can be seen not only in Kathmandu, Patan, and Bhaktapur, but also

Open courtyards often can provide a changing scene. Here in Thimi yarn is drying following the dyeing.

The roof of this temple is supported by struts carved in the greatest detail with mythical and erotic figures—Patan.

in the numerous villages throughout the valley. Unfortunately many of these fine works are now deteriorating.

Many factors made the Kathmandu Valley a leading center of art in Asia: the fine weather and natural resources, the major trade routes that created an affluent merchant class, and the concentration of wealth in the hands of the various rulers who patronized the arts. The Nepalese rulers made a lasting contribution by glorifying their deities in art and architecture.

Strolling through the ancient city of Bhaktapur, one of the three former city-states, one comes across a number of beautifully laid-out town squares with amazing temples, pagodas, and religious monuments. The labyrinth of streets and alleyways connecting the squares are fronted

by half-timbered brick houses with ornate facades and intricately carved window grills. This decorative detail was taken from the Muslim tradition, brought to Nepal by way of Moghul India. Time and weather have damaged these structures which, cracked and sinking, will be lost forever without immediate restoration.

Bhaktapur now is considered an historical and architectural monument. Donations from the German Cultural Society made it possible to restore many buildings, but the impressive restorations done in the early 1980s already show signs of deteriorating. The community of

Although abandoned now, one can observe the wonderfully executed details in the wood carving of this temple—Thimi, Kathmandu Valley.

Bhaktapur does not have the wealth to maintain its heritage, although the traditional culture is very much alive. Magnificent temples play an important part in the life of the city. However, the population will not be able to preserve these precious works without outside help.

In Patan, workshops still buzz with professional artists recreating traditional Buddhist and Hindu bronze statuary. The workers are descendents of the Newari artists, who were the leading Himalayan artists and whose influence was prominently felt in the region for centuries.

The production of traditional religious art is very much alive in Nepal today, both for local use in homes and tem-

Statuary abounds in the many plazas and squares of Patan. Here two bronze figures are the object of daily offerings.

This city square in Bhaktapur, used the previous week for the thrashing and winnowing of rice, is now being used for the throwing of pots.

The handicraft industry produces not only utilitarian objects—puppets are made for enacting historical and religious dramas.

ples and for export abroad. Here the time-consuming, lost-wax process is still used to create bronze metal sculpture. After the works are cast, they are hand finished to bring out the exquisite detail. The artists of Patan have preserved their ancestors' ability to evoke their deities through the graceful movements and fine lines of their sculptures. Although the Nepalese were originally influenced by the art of India, in their rendering of figures they left the Indian physical ideal behind and went on to develop an ideal of their own.[26,27]

In addition to small and large brass figures, a great variety of ceremonial objects are made, including lamps, masks, vases, and iconographically detailed hardware. Although much of the work produced in Patan might be considered handicrafts, the quality of the work puts it in the category of fine art.

An example of work on a lost wax brass figurine—here the young man is engraving the detail on the small Buddha statue—Patan.

The multitude of brass figurines and papier-mâché objects for sale are made as much for local religious and ceremonial functions as they are for export—Patan.

A woman in Ghoripani spinning wool.

Nepalese handicrafts industries continue to produce most of the items used for everyday life—pottery, basketry, carved wood products, jewelry, and woolen textiles, to name a few. Often this work is carried out by specific castes, continuing the traditions of their ancestors to produce beautiful objects of excellent quality (pages 78, 83).

Over the past two decades, several centers have been established in the Kathmandu and Pokara areas for the weaving of fine woolen rugs. These workshops are operated by Tibetan refugees who arrived in Nepal in the 1960s, following the Chinese takeover. The rugs are made in the traditional Tibetan style, using traditional designs. These small industries export rugs abroad and provide a modest income for many of the refugees.[28]

A large vessel is being shaped as the little girl learns a traditional craft from her father—Thimi.

Pots drying in the village square of Thimi.

Governance of Nepal

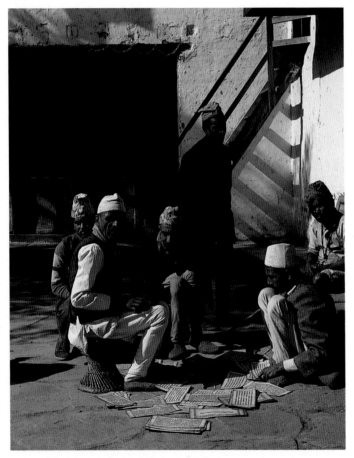

Government workers from the local council or panchayat are reviewing important records.

MOVEMENT TOWARDS DEMOCRACY proceeds slowly in Nepal, with its long history of autocratic rule. In the Spring of 1990, numerous strikes and riots took place throughout the country by forces endeavoring to establish a multi-party system based upon full democratic principles. These massive demonstrations and numerous deaths moved the King to agree to open talks leading to the development of a European style constitutional monarchy with a true multi-party system.

The present government came into existence as a result of a power struggle which lasted over a quarter of a century. After King Tribhuvan's authority was reestablished, the country experimented briefly with democracy. The King set up a coalition government, with the Nepal Congress Party (NCP) representing the majority of the people. In the newly established parliament, however, there was fighting between members of the Communist Party and the Ranas, who were trying to regain control. The situation was unstable, and the King declared a state of emergency, abolishing all parties to the extreme left and right, and forbidding political meetings and rallies. In 1954, the NCP boycotted the King's Advisory Assembly, strongly protesting that they were not allowed to set up the government even though they were the majority party. On his deathbed, the King dissolved the Council of State and passed all his power to his son, King Mahendra.

King Mahendra wanted a democratic government, but his efforts met with little success. He presented a new constitution and held nationwide elections for the Senate and

Lower House. In this first popular election, the NCP received the majority of the votes, thirty-eight percent. The election was considered successful in spite of the country's ninety-six percent illiteracy rate. The major flaw in the constitution was that the King still maintained all of the power, since he determined all civil rights.

In the newly elected parliament, clashes between the old Ranas and the NCP continued. The most important issue concerned land tenure and reform, with the Ranas, as large landowners, wanting to retain their land. The King was impatient with the functioning of parliament and lacked tolerance for dissent. He dissolved the parliament and jailed both the Rana and NCP party leaders. Rights under the constitution were abolished. The King put together a council of ministers whom he picked himself.

In 1961 King Mahendra established a *panchayat* (council) system of governance. At the bottom of this four-tiered system are the Village Councils, or *Gaon Sabhas*, whose members are freely elected by the citizens of the village. The village panchayat deals with problems related to local affairs, including education, sanitation, and health. Representatives from this council are sent to the next level, the District Panchayat, or *Zilla Sabhas*, which in turn elects representatives to the Zone Panchayat, or *Anchal Sabhas*. Each zone committee has an elected chairman; but each also has a zone commissioner who is appointed directly by the king and is a higher authority than the zone chairman.

From the Zone Panchayat, representatives are elected to the National Assembly, the *Rashtriya Panchayat* for a five-year term. There are 140 members on the Rashtriya, of whom 112 are elected through the panchayat system and the remainder appointed by the king. The prime minister, selected by the king, leads the Council of Ministers,

which carries out the responsibilities of the government. The ministers are appointed by the king, but are directly responsible to the Rashtriya Panchayat.

Committees of the Rashtriya, in consultation with the ministers, present various bills to the Rashtriya for consideration and passage, including the annual budget. Under the constitution the members enjoy freedom from arrest for anything they say in that body and can vote with impunity.

The major ministries of the Council of Ministers are as follows: Foreign Affairs and Land Reform; Works; Transportation and Communication; Panchayat and Local Government; Agriculture, Forest and Soil Conservation; Commerce; Health, Education and Culture; and Finance and Industry. There are a Supreme Court, four regional courts, fifteen zone courts, and seventy-five district courts—all of which have both civil and criminal jurisdiction. The Supreme Court has a Chief Justice and six additional justices. Although political parties are banned, both the Communist Party of Nepal and the Nepali Congress Party still maintain offices in Kathmandu. The King maintains a strong autocratic role at the top.

King Mahendra's son, Birendra, who came to power in 1972, encountered severe criticism of the panchayat system. Opposition leaders, demanding greater representation, were exiled or jailed, and student unrest was rife. A nonviolent movement against the government was begun, with opposition leaders advocating noncooperation. In 1979 the King held a referendum to allow the population to choose between multi-party system of government or the panchayat system, and the voters supported the panchayat system with 54.8 percent of the vote. This system has been in operation ever since, although the talks which the King agreed to in April 1990 increase the likelihood of democratization.

Part Three
LADAKH

*In spite of the harsh climate encountered above 13,000 feet,
this mother and child are healthy and robust.*

*This imposing chorten is situated outside the Shey Gompa.
The writings state the Buddhist mantra: Om Mani Padme Hum.*

The Land

ALTHOUGH LADAKH IS UNIQUE topographically and culturally, it is difficult to find on most maps of Asia. Pakistan is to the north, Kashmir to the west, India to the south, and Chinese-occupied Tibet to the east—but exact borders appear amorphous. Asking for information about Ladakh's precise geographic position, one is usually told how to get there. Transportation into this remote area by any other means than foot or animal was not possible until the end of World War II, when the Indian government hastily built a road to stave off the Chinese encroachment on one of its borders and the invasion of Pakistani forces on another (page 92).

Today the journey from Srinagar, Kashmir, to Leh, Ladakh's capital, requires two days of driving over three high, winding passes, climbing to almost 13,000 feet (page 92). The road was opened to tourists in 1974. The first civilian air flights landed in Leh in 1979. Ancient routes leading over the high mountain passes into Tibet and along the Brahmaputra River were closed following border conflicts with China, and are now heavily guarded by the Indian Army on one side and the Chinese Army on the other.

Politically Ladakh is now a district of the Indian state of *Jammu* and *Kashmir*. Although kingdoms do not legally exist in India, Ladakh's royal family is very much in evidence, playing a leading role in local politics and socio-economic affairs. The "Queen" was formerly a member of the Indian Parliament.

Nestled amidst three mountain ranges—the Great Hi-malayan and Zanskar ranges to the south, and the Karakoram range to the north—Ladakh occupies the extremely broad valley of the Indus River and a number of smaller valleys as well (pages 93, 94, 95). The largest proportion of the population resides in the Indus valley and the hills overlooking it. The total area of Ladakh is approximately 60,000 square miles (about the size of Iowa), but one-third of this land lies in Aksai Chin in Chinese-occupied Tibet, and a mere one-half of one percent of the land is arable.

With an average altitude of 19,000 feet Ladakh is one of the highest areas of the world where the population lives by means of agriculture and the culture is still intact. The majority of the population lives between 10,000 and 13,000 feet, surrounded by mountains that reach up to 24,000 feet. In addition to the extreme altitude, Ladakh's climate is one of the harshest to which a population group has learned to adapt and still sustain a rich culture. Here the winters are frigid day and night; the summers are blazing in the daytime, but still freezing at night; and the average rainfall is only about three inches a year.

When the British explorer Alexander Cunningham first visited Ladakh in 1846, he stated: "The general aspect of Ladakh is extreme barrenness. Seen from above, the country would appear a mere succession of yellow plains and barren mountains capped with snow. No trace of man nor of human habitation would meet the eye; and even the large spots of cultivated land would be but small specks on the mighty waste of deserted world."[29] The land

Looking beyond the jagged Stok Range one can see the broad Indus River Valley.

Main road goes over the Zoji-La Pass (11,500 feet) before reaching Leh.

looks the same today. Some even compare Ladakh's un-cannily stark and rugged beauty to the landscape of the moon. If it weren't for the mighty Indus River flowing through the heart of the country and the glacial water streaming down from permanently snowcapped mountains, it would indeed be an uninhabitable, treeless wasteland (pages 96, 97).

Over the centuries the Ladakhis have developed ingenious ways to irrigate their crops. In the narrow valleys where the streams flow down to meet the Indus River, and along the broad Indus valley itself, these resourceful people have engineered a system of terraces and small canals. Built with the ever-present supply of stones, they provide an abundance of water in spite of the lack of rainfall. With the brilliant sunshine and cloudless skies of this altitude, crops grow quickly. During the short summer season, wherever there is human habitation, vibrant swatches of green barley can be seen growing in the terraces. Surprisingly, there are even small apple and apricot trees at this extreme elevation. In order to maintain their almost total self-sufficiency, the Ladakhis dry the produce from their summer harvest to ensure ample reserves for the long winter.

At this altitude and extreme cold temperature, the conifers usually associated with high mountains don't grow. A small number of poplar, willow, and tamarisk trees do grow along the riverbanks, however, and these are greatly valued. Their timber is reserved for the rafters and roofing of the sturdy, well-built Ladakhi homes. Wood is too precious to be used as fuel; yak dung provides the main fuel source here.

Ladakh was virtually cut off from the surrounding world until recently, though historically the country lay at the crossroads between Central Asia, India, and Tibet.

Muddy Zanskar River along the route to Leh blends in with the desert scenery.

As one enters Ladakh from Kashmir a fertile valley comes into sight, breaking up the bleakness of the barren mountains.

Near the Indus River a tributary stream irrigates a fertile valley.

The air approach to Leh from Srinagar takes one over the impressive Nun Kun Mountains of the Zanskar Range, situated at approximately 23,500 feet.

Limited communication with the outside world was mainly provided by traders who came to exchange wares for such items as yak wool, by pilgrims en route to or from Tibet, and by the many military incursions from east and west. Consequently, the Ladakhi people learned to survive, perhaps thrive, on their paucity of natural resources. Any available resources were remarkably well used; almost nothing was wasted. The ecological balance between land and people was highly effective, providing for basic human needs without incurring any perceptible degradation of the environment.

Now that Ladakh has become of interest to tourists, and communication with the outside world has improved, there is a significant threat to the delicate ecological balance which has existed here for centuries. Ecologists are concerned that even small changes in the attitudes and behavior of the people—particularly changes that affect their lifestyle and land use—can have long-term, devastating effects. Efforts are being made to help the Ladakhis maintain the basic fabric of their culture, while at the same time introducing the most appropriate technology to provide them with a better life.

The trail to the Markham Valley takes one over Stok La Pass.

People of Ladakh

A peasant woman with a stovepipe hat.

BEFORE THE NINETEENTH CENTURY, Ladakh was an active and vital center for the ancient trade routes of Central Asia, including Chinese Turkestan, India, and Tibet. The silk route merchants traversed Ladakh, going north to Yarkand and Kashgar, where the main route went east to Beijing and west to Venice. Caravans from every direction traveled through the capital city of Leh, carrying staple items and riches from all over Asia, and even from Europe. The coral that Ladakhi women wore in their headdresses, for instance, came from the Mediterranean.

Unlike the more fertile Nepal or Bhutan, Ladakh was able to entice few traders or pilgrims on their way to Lhasa to remain. The inhospitable terrain and climate made Ladakh a most unlikely destination. The settlers who did find Ladakh to their liking came mainly from neighboring mountain kingdoms. The scarcity of natural resources required that those who stayed have the ability to survive and the stamina to endure. The hardy Ladakhi settlers, in fact, did far more than just survive. They managed to thrive in their own inimitable way.

History is vague on the subject, but the earliest people to settle in Ladakh were the *Mons*. They were Buddhists who practiced a more traditional form of the religion than the tantric practices of Tibetan Buddhism. Some evidence of their architecture stands. Today Mons tribesmen can still be found in Ladakh. They work as carpenters, and also serve as musicians, performing in the villages during the religious festivals.

The traditional stovepipe hat is a frequent sight in Ladakh.

A Ladakhi family, with their son, a young monk, home from the monastery.

The *Dards*, another mountain people, migrated to Ladakh from the Hindu Kush mountains in the west. Precisely when they arrived is not certain, but it was long enough ago for them to be mentioned by the Greek historian Herodotus (484–425 B.C.E.) and by Alexander the Great (336–323 B.C.E.). An agrarian group, the Dards are of Indo-European stock—some have fair skin and blue eyes. They settled in the Dras, Hanu and Da valleys in the western part of the kingdom. While a few Dards still practice Buddhism, the majority converted to Islam three centuries ago.

There was regular travel and communication between Ladakh and Tibet in ancient times. Most of the Ladakhi population are descendents of Tibetan nomads who wandered westward from Tibet, grazing their animals in the fertile niches along the way. When this migration began is not known. The land itself did not differ significantly from the western parts of Tibet, so the nomads' methods of coping with scarcity of resources and brutal weather were already tried and true. For those who settled, the concept of a border between Tibet and Ladakh did not exist. As they migrated westward, they brought with them their own religion and culture. Ladakhis of Tibetan origin are still the majority of the inhabitants living along the Indus River, although a significant number of Muslim traders also settled in the Indus valley (page 99).

Other groups of people have arrived in Ladakh more recently. Many from other parts of India are in commerce or serve as government officials. Especially noticeable at Leh, the capital, are the Kashmiri merchants, most of whom are Muslim. They do a brisk business selling souvenirs and generally catering to the increasing numbers of tourists. More experienced in trade than the easy-going Ladakhis, the Kashmiris excel in marketing and hence dominate the marketplace. The Ladakh winters are too severe for them, however, and every year they retreat to their homes in Kashmir, at lower elevations.

Camped along the Chinese and Pakistani borders, in the Indus Valley, and at other key places is the Indian Army. It was sent to secure the country from invasion. The military are present in sufficient numbers (approximately 40,000) to have a major impact on the local population. Because Ladakh's resources are sufficient only for the survival of the local inhabitants, the Army has had to import most of its provisions from India. Of course, some of the Indian food and material goods have found their way into Ladakhi homes. Traditionally self-sufficient, the Ladakhis have begun to grow dependent upon imported foods and household items. Likewise, living near the soldiers, most of whom are Hindu, is having some effect on the local culture. Still, there is little evidence of conflict, and the Indian Army tends to keep a low profile in the area.

Buddhism rejects the use of status to separate people, yet this practice has been a part of Ladakhi society throughout its history. Among the people of Tibetan origin, there is a social structure based on class and caste. Unlike the theocratic social structure that was in effect in Buddhist Tibet, Ladakh has been a monarchy with a class

This Muslim man works in the wool gathering trade—Kargil.

A well-stocked tourist shop operated by Kashmiris.

structure. Although this system is breaking down as India democratizes the country, significant aspects of it are still alive. Some of the Ladakhis' elitist attitudes are rationalized by their tantric beliefs. The upper social strata think that the lower-caste people are responsible for disturbing the earth spirits, thus there is justification for treating them as outcastes.

Traditionally the royalty, or *Rgyal-Rigs*, has been at the top of the class structure; followed by the nobility, or *Sku-*

Drag; then the commoners, or *Dmans-Rigs*. At the bottom of the structure, which is akin to the caste system, are the *Mgar-ba*, *Mon*, and *Be-da*, in that order. The Mgar-ba caste are blacksmiths, and they are allowed to own property. So, too, are the Mons. The Be-da, the lowest caste, cannot own property. They follow the Islamic faith and are beggars and wandering minstrels. These low-caste people are considered impure and a source of pollution. There are strict taboos against eating food pre-

A view over a typical rural Ladakhi village situated at about 13,000 feet.

The traditional Ladakhi headdress is covered with large turquoise stones. Family wealth is often measured by the size and number of stones.

Ladakhis take great pride in their kitchens.

Almost total self-sufficiency is necessary for the Ladakhi family living in this isolated, well-built home.

pared by them, having sexual relations with them, or even touching them.[30]

Even with democracy as the rule of the land, remnants of the old system persist. Although those of royal or noble lineage no longer rule, members of the royal family continue to play leadership roles in the country. Accumulated wealth has replaced nobility as the primary criterion of high rank. The greater one's wealth, the better his education, and the better his position. Another factor that tends to perpetuate this system is the tendency of Ladakhis to marry within their own social group.

Ladakh's population remained relatively stable from the early nineteenth century, when the first census was taken, until recently. Between 1975 and 1985, however, the population has increased thirty percent, from 100,000 to 130,000. One explanation for the former stability was the practice of sending a significant number of young boys of each generation to become monks. An-

The streets of Leh are narrow, often filled with people of many ethnic backgrounds.

Ladakhi men in local garb.

Housing in Leh around small courtyard.

other common tradition was the practice of fraternal polyandry, wherein one or more brothers would be wedded to the same woman. Each of the brothers would carry responsibility for the wife and the children that resulted from the unions. While unusual by western standards, this arrangement had a number of very practical results. It kept the family house and lands intact and, since many women would remain unmarried and childless, it kept the birthrate low. The eldest son would inherit the home and land, and the younger ones would share in the labor and produce. The recent trend is away from sending young boys to become monks, and there has been a decline in polyandry, as it is now forbidden by the government. These factors seem now to have driven the population upward.

There are many favorable accounts of the excellent social traits of the Ladakhi people and their success as a group in creating a humanistic and congenial society. Travelers to the area frequently comment on the inhabitants' compelling good nature. A resilient country folk, they are hospitable, trustworthy, and honest. Singing and laughing while working in the fields, regardless of physical hardships, they give a strong impression of really enjoying life. Their Buddhist faith promotes a deeply spiritual nature and a characteristic appreciation of the moment.

In the rhythm of the seasons, summer is a time of intense agricultural activity—planting, growing, and harvesting. Much of the productivity necessary for survival occurs during these few months. Houses and terraces must also be built and repaired, and food must be dried and stored to be ready for the winter months (page 103).

The brutal winter climate imposes severe limitations on the Ladakhi lifestyle, thus promoting closeness between family members of all ages. Winter finds the entire family inside, often huddled around the fireplaces and stoves. There is plenty of time for storytelling and game playing. With three or four generations under one roof, there is a continuous transmission of culture and religious beliefs. The main source of fuel for heat and cooking, is dung from the yak, *dzo*, or other animals (page 102).[31]

The diet of the Ladakhi family varies little. Toasted barley meal, called *tsampa*, is made into small cakes that are eaten cooked or uncooked. Butter tea, made of yak butter churned with tea and salt, is a mainstay. This brew is more acceptable to outsiders when thought of as broth rather than tea. During the summer, a variety of fruits and leafy vegetables are available. Only small amounts of meat are eaten. Buddhists are not supposed to kill animals, so the only meat eaten, by and large, is that of animals killed by accident or at the hands of non-Buddhists. Of course, due to outside influences, new foods are slowly entering the Ladakhi diet.

At first glance, outsiders may regard the Ladakhis as primitive, and certainly Ladakh is one of the few places left in the world where one can see life as it was before the Industrial Revolution. But there are many extremely civilized elements in this mountain culture. Most Ladakhis live in commodious houses, often three stories high. Both men and women dress in attractive homespun fabrics and wear stunning jewelry. And, most significantly, the balance the Ladakhis have established between fulfilling their communal needs and using nature's resources is highly sophisticated.

Until recently Ladakh's fragile environment remained unscathed, despite the intensive farming. But today, changes are taking place which are threatening this balance and breaking down the traditional patterns.

History of Ladakh

SQUEEZED TIGHTLY BETWEEN Tibet and Kashmir, the Kingdom of Ladakh was continuously influenced by the actions of its aggressive neighbors. Its religion, language, and culture were predominantly influenced by Tibet and dominated politically by Kashmir.

As in the case of Bhutan, pre-eighteenth century accounts of Ladakh are rare. The texts that do exist are mostly the scholarly writings of the lamas, who were more interested in matters of religion than in political or temporal events. Early history does reveal that a serious religious and political upheaval took place in Tibet in the ninth century, and the Tibetan king tried to eradicate all traces of Buddhism there and return the country to the animistic practices of Bon. At that time the Tibetan Prince Nomagoan, a Buddhist, fled to Ladakh where he set himself up as king, and established the Buddhist faith and monasteries there. It is ironic that China's recent attempt to wipe out Buddhism in Tibet has had a similar effect: it caused the fourteenth Dalai Lama to flee, and as a result Tibetan Buddhism is beginning to flourish throughout the world.

At the time of King Nomagoan, Ladakh was thought of as Western Tibet, and it became a leading center for Buddhism. During his reign, the King extended his kingdom beyond the present borders into Kashmir, Zanskar, and Baltistan, and turned back the Mongol warriors who were raiding from Central Asia. His capital was at Shey, near Leh, in the Indus Valley.

Upon Nomagoan's death, as was the custom, the extensive kingdom was divided among his three sons, with Spal-Gyi-Gon receiving the portion that corresponds to present-day Ladakh. Under the new Ladakhi king, Buddhism flowered. The king brought scholars and artisans from India to establish monasteries and Buddhist artists from Kashmir to decorate the monastery at Alchi. A generation later in Tibet, Bon was again displaced by Buddhism, and the Ladakhis once more looked to Tibet as the cultural and spiritual center of Buddhism.

In 1337 Kashmir fell to a Muslim dynasty. Its rulers did their best to wipe away any traces of Hinduism and Buddhism. Islam continued to spread eastward, and by the end of the fifteenth century Ladakh was surrounded on the south and west by states that had converted to the Islamic religion. Gradually people were converting to Islam even in the valleys on the western border of central Ladakh. Tibetan-speaking peoples in the valleys of the Suru and Indus rivers were now praying towards Mecca.

In the sixteenth century, the Namgyal Dynasty began in Ladakh, with the reign of Sovang Namgyal, and held power for over four centuries. Sovang Namgyal excelled as both a conqueror and an administrator. During his reign, he moved the capitol to Leh and extended his territory deep into the heart of Tibet and far to the west. He constructed roads and bridges, easing the difficulties of travel across the rugged terrain. The next several generations of Namgyal rulers built numerous monasteries. Large mani walls were constructed, many of which stand today.

The Ladakhi boundaries were unsettled at this time, with Ladakh constantly seeking either to conquer or regain land from its neighbors. On one occasion Leh was captured by forces of the Indian Moghul Emperor in Delhi. The Ladakhi king, Deldan Namgyal, made peace by converting to Islam himself and allowing the Islamic religion also to be practiced in Ladakh. A mosque was built in the main square of Leh, directly below his palace. This edifice is still in use. In the following generations, the Namgyal kings continued to pay homage to the Muslim rulers of India (page 109).

In the last part of the seventeenth century, Ladakh was the site of a bloody clash between the Tibetan-Mongol army and the army of the great Moghul king of India, Aurangzeb. Ladakh had refused to accept the Gelug-pa school of Buddhism, headed by Tibet's fifth Dalai Lama. The Dalai Lama was insistent, and a Holy War ensued. Ladakh was invaded by Tibet. To drive out the Tibetan invaders, Ladakh's king brought in the Moghul army—and indeed the Moghuls routed the Tibetan-Mongol forces, pushing them far back across the border into Tibet. In the end, however, rather than see his people forcibly converted to Islam, the head lama of Ladakh agreed to accept the Gelug-pa school of the Dalai Lama. The following generations of Ladakhi kings were weak, and affairs of heart were often put above the affairs of state. In fact, several rulers in a row were regarded as mad.

From 1834 to 1841 Ladakh was engaged in an all-out struggle to maintain its separateness from the Sikh state of Jammu and Kashmir under its Dogra ruler, Maharaja Gulab Singh. The Maharaja, with the permission of the British, marched 5,000 men into Ladakh. Putting up stiff resistance, Ladakh finally capitulated and became a vassal state. The Maharaja's commander, Zorawar, entered Leh to work out the terms of peace, and then left the country to conquer Zanskar.

Meanwhile, displeased with the settlement, Ladakh decided to struggle for independence and began to raise its own army. Learning of this, Zorawar marched his army back into Leh and squelched the revolt. Ladakh's king was banished to the palace at Stok, but was reinstated after he and his ministers agreed to pay hefty fines. Following the king's death, his son Hijmed Singe Namgyal came to power. He accepted the permanent domination of the Dogras over Ladakh, and agreed to pay an annual tribute to the Maharaja.

For the next 106 years, until 1947, Ladakh remained under Dogra domination. Eventually the royal family was deposed, although they were given the Stok Palace as their residence, where they still live today. The Dogra army continued to occupy Leh, and a succession of governors was appointed by the Maharaja of Jammu to rule the kingdom.

The military conflicts were not over, however. Ladakh continued to be caught in the middle of a brutal war between the Dogras of Jammu and the King of Tibet. The Dogra army, under General Zorawar, swept through Ladakh and into Tibet, advancing almost to Lhasa. Along the way they looted and pillaged everywhere, stripping the monasteries of their rich art and treasures. In 1841 the Tibetans counter-attacked and inflicted severe damage on the Dogras, killing Zorawar.

Crippled by the extreme Himalayan winter, the Dogras took devastating punishment. In the spring, pursued by vengeful Tibetans, they retreated all the way to Ladakh. There, on the verge of being driven out of Ladakh entirely, the Dogras saved themselves by secretly diverting a nearby stream into the Tibetan campsite. The Tibetan army was caught off guard by the resulting flood. They surrendered and a treaty was signed, which left the Ladakh border intact.

After India achieved independence in 1947, Ladakh became a district of the State of Jammu and Kashmir, and since then Ladakh has been administered by an Indian District Commissioner. Even in this modern era, however, the country has been subject to continuing invasions by its hostile neighbors to the east and west.

In October of 1947 the newly established nation of Pakistan, dissatisfied at having lost most of Kashmir to India, attacked and occupied parts of Indian Kashmir. Its forces advanced as far as Kargil and held the pass at Zojila, on the border of Ladakh. Ladakh was now effectively isolated, cut off from Kashmir entirely. The Gilgit Scouts of Pakistan advanced down the Indus River, coming within twelve miles of Leh. The Indian Army, however, quickly built an airstrip at the foot of Shey Monastery near Leh. Soon Indian planes began to land with reinforcements, and the Muslim forces of Pakistan were routed from the valley and pushed out of Indian Kashmir.

On October 20, 1959, Ladakh was invaded by the Chinese forces that invaded Tibet. A large but isolated section of the country, Aksai Chin, was taken and is still held by the Chinese. China believes it has a "historical" claim to Ladakh because it has a "historical" claim to Tibet; therefore, China feels its annexation of Aksai Chin is justified. Indian and Chinese troops continue to face one another across the well-patrolled and tense border of Ladakh and Aksai Chin. Neither side regards the border issue as settled.

The border conflict with Pakistan is equally unsettled. In the summers of 1986 and 1987, for example, fighting broke out between Indian and Pakistani troops to the northwest of Ladakh. The routes from Ladakh to Tibet are now closed, and all of Ladakh's commerce and communication is with India and the western world. Nevertheless, Ladakhis continue to look to Tibet for spiritual inspiration, as embodied in the person of the Dalai Lama. In 1987, they built a summer retreat facility for him along the Indus River to the east of Leh.

The long-standing tensions between the Ladakhi Buddhists and the Kashmiri Muslims erupted anew in 1989. The administrators of the local government programs for Ladakh have been consistently appointed from the ranks of Muslims by the Jammu and Kashmir State Government. Although in recent years more Ladakhis have received a higher education and are in the civil service, the most important posts continue to be filled by Kashmiri Muslims. This kind of political and economic discrimination, along with the strong separatist movement among the Kashmiris demanding unification with Pakistan, had heightened the tensions in Leh.

The frustration felt by the Ladakhis led to an outbreak of violence between the Buddhists and the Muslims in Leh in August of 1989. A number of Buddhists were killed by police attempting to quell the disturbance. Following this there was a mass protest march and a strike. The Government arrested many Ladakhis and established a curfew. The Ladakhi Buddhists, who comprise an eighty-four percent majority of the population in this region, fear increased domination from Kashmir. The Ladakh People's Movement, as a result of these concerns and fears of Islamic militancy, is strongly advocating that Ladakh become a separate territory ruled from New Delhi rather than Srinagar.

The main mosque in Leh is situated below the old royal palace in the town square.

Religion in Ladakh

At the Shey Gompa stands a gigantic prayer wheel. A young lad appears with two ceremonial trumpets.

R EMOTE, MASSIVE MONASTERIES clinging to steep cliffsides; rows of worn, white-plastered chortens in the blazing sun; deeply engraved mani stones stretching like punctuation marks across the ridge of a hill—all these tell visitors to Ladakh that they have entered a spiritual land. The silhouettes of these sacred symbols against the sky are constant reminders of this country's deep reverence for the Buddha. And while these Buddhist images are totally captivating, one needs to remember that Ladakh is also a stronghold of Islam, even though its symbols are less conspicuous (page 88).

Buddhism first came to Ladakh from India shortly after the life of the Buddha, although few records remain from this period. Later, Buddhism came to Ladakh directly from Tibet. As in Bhutan, teachers of many schools of Buddhism arrived and established monasteries and seats of learning. Unlike Bhutan, however, one lineage has never dominated the others, and as a result, several schools exist today, each with its own head lama and monasteries.

The first to arrive from Tibet was the lineage that follows the teachings of Guru Padmasambhava, the great teacher who spread Buddhism into Tibet and Bhutan. This is the *Nyingma* school, which had its early beginnings in India. Today it maintains a monastery at Thakthak. Next came the *Kagyu* lineage, which eventually split into the *Drigung* and *Drukpa* schools, with major monasteries at Lamayuru and Hemis.[32]

The Red Hats and Yellow Hats are the two remaining major groups in the panoply of Buddhist schools here.

A row of chortens facing across the Indus River Valley.

Storage of holy texts and ceremonial trumpets while not in use.

The "Red Hat" or *Sakya* order was previously the more important of the two; but it gave way to the "Yellow Hat" or *Gelug* order, a reform movement dating from the fifteenth century whose principal monasteries are at Spituk and Tikse. After the Dalai Lama, the head of the Gelug order, fled from Tibet in 1959, the lamas at Tikse sought a close affiliation with him, and as a result, the Dalai Lama makes his summer home near Tikse (page 113).

Although it is fortunate that so many small enclaves of the Tibetan Buddhist tradition are alive in Ladakh, the survival of so many different orders has caused an economic strain. Since the religion is not supported by the state, the many groups, each with its own ancient monastic buildings filled with precious works of art, must survive on their own. With only a small population to support them, their continued existence is threatened. The monasteries here, unlike those in Bhutan, are in a poor state of repair. Recently they have started charging tourists small admission fees so that restoration can begin.

To the outsider, the many orders are not all that discernibly different from one another. The schools vary less in their teachings than in the esoteric details pertaining to their origins. What is clearly of importance is the fact that their message, the principles taught by the Buddha, has created what might be called the Ladakhi character: tranquility, selflessness, and compassion for all living things.

There are considerable similarities between the religious practices and rituals of Bhutan and Ladakh. Boys of both countries are still sent off to the lamaseries at an early age to become monks. The importance of accumulating merit through making offerings and reciting the sacred mantras is the same. Even the annual ceremonies and dances are quite alike. However, the monasteries of Ladakh seem infinitely more remote and austere. The original meaning of *gompa* or monastery was "a remote place for meditation." In Ladakh, several of the principal gompas are far removed from the populated areas and barely accessible.[34]

The monasteries at Alchi, Tikse, and Hemis are among the most important and beautiful. Alchi is the oldest. Located on the main route between Srinagar and Leh, it was founded by a Tibetan nobleman in the eleventh century. Although the monastery itself is hardly used today, it is famous for the beautifully rendered murals that adorn its walls. These supreme examples of the period's art survived only because Alchi had been abandoned in the sixteenth century. By the time the Muslims rampaged through Ladakh destroying all traces of Buddhism, this ancient monastery had long been closed and forgotten, and thus it escaped destruction. Its murals, created by Kashmiri Buddhist artists, depict a combination of sacred and mythical themes and represent the only extant example of this superbly elaborate style of painting.[35,36]

Not far down the Indus River from Leh is the Tikse Gompa, a massive structure that sits on a steep hillside. It overlooks a small village at its base and, beyond that, the fertile Indus Valley with its expansive barley fields. Built in the fifteenth century, Tikse is the principal gompa in the region and the seat of the Gelug order. The monastery continues to expand: in 1980 a new wing was constructed and was consecrated by the Dalai Lama. Inside there is a lofty statue of Buddha sitting in the lotus position (page 116).

Further down the river and up in a small wooded gorge is the Hemis Monastery, the largest and most prosperous gompa in Ladakh. It was established in the early seven-

The Tikse Monastery complex clustered around a hill.

An older lama of the Tikse Monastery.

On the road to Leh one passes the impressive ancient Lamaruyu Gompa.

The central square and main place of worship at Lamaruyu.

This large Buddha, just a few years old, was dedicated to the current Dalai Lama.

teenth century in a highly sacred spot, and is still a major pilgrimage site and the location of the most important religious festival in Ladakh. The Hemis Festival, a two-day affair, is akin to the Mani Rimdu in Nepal and the Wangdi Tshechu in Bhutan. During this event, the monks perform ancient masked dances which enact the struggles between the primeval forces of good and evil. Every twelfth year a gigantic embroidered thangka is unrolled in the courtyard, with sewn images of Guru Padmasambhava and other saints.

The Muslim population of Ladakh is centered in two areas: around Kargil to the west, and in and around Leh. The Muslims in the Kargil region are of the *Shiite* order, which is centered in Iraq. These Muslims are known for their extreme orthodoxy. They follow a strict code of behavior, refraining from alcohol, gambling, music, and even the traditional local sport of polo. The Muslim community in Leh is part of the *Sunni* branch. Its members are less strict in their observance. Many are merchants who have immigrated from Kashmir. Marriage between Sunnis and Buddhists in Leh is not uncommon.

Isolated from the outside world, young monks at Hemis Monastery are only too happy to make contact.

Ladakhi Arts and Crafts

Y THE FIRST CENTURY C.E., several advanced civilizations had flowered in the lower Indus Valley, spreading their influence and artwork throughout Ladakh. Ladakh was the first of the three kingdoms to gaze upon the earliest statues of the Buddha. This Gandharan sculpture—a style of Greco-Roman origins—depicted the Buddha with Hellenistic features, his torso covered with a toga that showed his bodily contours, narrowed hips and broad shoulders. Later, around the fifth century, the Gupta style of art from southern and eastern regions of India came into Ladakh. These two styles helped to shape early Ladakhi art.

Situated at the crossroads of Asia, Ladakh was on the "Silk Road" and had famous Buddhist centers to the north and the south. The trade routes through it were widely used for well over a thousand years. During that time, travelers commonly bartered small bronze sculptures and thangkas for local commodities and services. It was only natural that this artwork, which was carried into the marketplaces and monasteries of Ladakh from all sides, have a lasting effect on the indigenous art.

In the seventh century, Tibetan and Nepalese artists began to have direct contact with Ladakh. Their work was heavily influenced by the stylized art of India. In the eighth century, the major outside influence came from Kashmir, which at that time was still Buddhist. The Kashmiris had evolved a style of sculpture and painting, less dependent upon the Indian heritage, which reflected the natural environment of plants and animals. This creative

Traditional art continues in Ladakh. Here a monk sculptor is nearing completion of the arm of a gigantic statue of the Buddha—Hemis Monastery.

A first century figure of Buddha carved on a rock situated behind a more recent religious structure.

trend was perhaps stimulated by the natural beauty of the Valley of Kashmir. Examples of this style can still be seen on the walls of the eleventh-century monastery in Alchi. The exuberant Kashmiri painting contrasted sharply with the more formal, Indian-influenced Nepalese and Tibetan art.

All these styles were added to the rich blend of local art. According to Singh Madanjeet, there began to be such a thorough cross-fertilization of artistic ideas in the region, that the artwork produced after the eleventh century could no longer be distinguished by geographic origin or style.[37] A variety of different syntheses evolved: in one studio an artist might have been copying centuries-old classical models, merely modifying some of the iconographic details; in another workshop, the sculptor might have been using the newer styles, combining artistic ideas from several different parts of the Himalayas.

By the fifteenth century, Kashmir had been largely converted to Islam and was a Muslim state. Its armies repeatedly raided Ladakh, vandalizing monasteries and, wherever possible, defacing Buddhist murals and other art. In the seventeenth century, the great Moghul ruler of India, Aurangzeb, gained control of Kashmir; as a result, Ladakh came under his rule as well. A puritanical Muslim, he forbade the depiction of the human figure in visual art. From this period on, there was a decline in the production of the larger murals, thangkas, and sculptures. Artists began to work only in smaller forms that could be kept hidden.

The great outpouring of sacred art, created to embellish the monasteries and aid the way to meditative insight and peace, is a thing of the past. Today the monasteries are museums of fine works of the Buddhist iconography developed in Ladakh which incorporates much of the tantric symbolism and detail of Tibetan Buddhism.

Unlike Nepal, Ladakh today produces little if any quality artwork for export. Most of the traditional art used for religious purposes is still made by local artists, but it is made for domestic use. Sculptors continue to complete large statues for the monasteries. Painters produce fine thangkas for the sacred shrines and for religious use in private homes. And local silversmiths craft small metal pieces such as bells, *dorjes*, and *phurbas* for religious ceremonies. These skills have not been lost and undoubtedly will be passed on to future generations because of their continuing religious significance. But it is illegal to take religious art out of Ladakh, and so there is no mass production to meet outside demand.

Handicrafts are another area of Ladakhi art and are subject to different regulations. A variety of artifacts is produced by local craftsmen. Ladakhis take great pride in the copperware that can be found in all their kitchens. And like the Bhutanese, Ladakhis weave the woolen material used for their regional dress. Both men and women participate in this cottage industry, which produces a distinctive high-quality cloth dyed in dark colors. Women's jewelry and headgear are of special importance in Ladakh. Like their Tibetan counterparts, Ladakhi women wear large necklaces of turquoise, coral, and silver. The stones are left in a rough state and are prized according to their size. Their earrings are mostly of pearl.

A large statue of Buddha with an ornately embellished headdress.

Courtyard at Hemis Monastery is surrounded by balconies, providing numerous places to view the annual festival.

The most outstanding feature of the women's costume is the *perak*, a long, lambskin hood covered with rows of precious and semi-precious jewels, predominantly turquoise. The size and number of stones on a woman's perak are a good indication of her family's wealth. The origin of the perak is unknown, but it is similar to the headgear worn by the Kalish or Kaffiri women of Pakistan, except that the Pakistani headgear is sewn with small conch shells instead of stones. The perak is often considered an heirloom and handed down from generation to generation.

Men and women both wear long, heavy, draped woolen gowns, tied at the waist. These robes are worn both summer and winter. Women almost always carry a shawl of shaggy white sheepskin draped over their backs. With their long, braided hair, heavy jewelry, and ornate headpieces, their appearance is stunning.

In Leh, a government-sponsored handicraft center produces items that can be legally brought out of the district. Most of these are woven or knitted goods. The value of the center is that it trains the local population in handicraft skills. The export items themselves, however, are expensive and of lower quality than the products made for local use.

Ladakhi women displaying their magnificent turquoise-studded peraks.

Governance of Ladakh

LADAKH IS DIVIDED INTO two administrative districts, both within the Indian State of Jammu and Kashmir. The Leh district has a population of approximately 60,000, and the Kargil district has a population of 50,000. The latter also includes what used to comprise the Kingdom of Zanskar. Although Ladakh is under the jurisdiction of the Jammu and Kashmir state government and is subject to state laws and policies, the central government of India plays a highly significant and visible role in the administration of its affairs. Since Ladakh is a remote frontier area and has been engaged in ongoing border disputes with both China and Pakistan, India has stationed several contingents of military there—which automatically necessitates a special relationship with the central government.

Before Ladakh was established as a part of a state of modern India, the most important issues of government were handled locally. With the villages remote from one another and from any central control, local leadership was required to solve local problems. Today many of the important day-to-day problems are still dealt with by the local villagers and the village headman (*godpa*), a position which usually rotates yearly among the villagers. Issues such as water distribution through the canals, the protection of agricultural lands from animals, and the preservation of trees are quite important and are dealt with by traditional means.

Ladakhis elect representatives to the state legislative body in Srinagar, the governmental seat for Jammu and Kashmir. Muslims, however, predominate in the state legislature. Ladakhis are invariably outvoted in issues related to differences in the Muslim and Buddhist value systems.

Many Ladakhis resent the controls from the government of Jammu and Kashmir, and desire direct rule from New Delhi. There have been lobbying efforts to give them a *Scheduled Tribe Status*, which would then allow them to receive special benefits and opportunities allowed other minority groups in India.

The major outside influence on Ladakhi affairs comes from programs sponsored by the central government of India. New Delhi appoints a District Commissioner (D.C.) for a two-year term to manage and coordinate governmental activities in Ladakh. The D.C. is selected from a pool of civil service officials trained by the central government. The number of departments and special programs financed and run by the government is high, and their effects are increasingly felt.

Due to the special status of Ladakh, the amount of money spent on these programs far exceeds the per capita expenditures for other Indian states. Even so, Ladakhis are not required to pay taxes. Consequently, they have come to take this largess for granted, expecting the government to take care of each new need as it becomes recognized. This contains the seed of a future problem: if they do not participate in their government, these historically independent, self-sufficient people could lose their ability to solve problems for themselves.

Several of the D.C.'s programs deal with the quantity and quality of food production. India sends in technical experts who introduce new ways of farming and raising livestock. Often these methods have been developed elsewhere, perhaps in tropical parts of India, and they frequently incorporate chemical technologies that are not appropriate for Ladakh's delicate ecosystem. Although the "modern" techniques may provide short-term benefits, the long-term consequences are not good. For instance, for a thousand years the Ladakhis have successfully fertilized their fields with night soil. With the introduction of inorganic chemical fertilizers there is now, for the first time, a risk of soil degradation. Similarly, Ladakhis have recently been encouraged to use pesticides on their leafy crops, even though few if any harmful pests are common to Ladakh. As a result, poisons have been introduced into the food chain.

One of the major divisions under the D.C. is the Power Department. This department has recently completed a dam at Stakna, up the valley from Leh, on the Indus River. The electricity project is meant to reduce the use of the petroleum-fueled generators that have, until now, supplied power to the villages in the Leh district, thus reducing the threat of air pollution in the valley. Practically speaking, however, although the dam will provide an adequate supply of power during the summer, when the river freezes in the winter the Ladakhis will still need to burn animal dung or buen petroleum. New power lines have been added to serve more villages, but at least initially, the villagers have little need for electricity. They continue to use the more traditional source of energy, animal dung, for their cooking and heating needs. Ecologists are also concerned that the availability of cheap energy will have long-term negative effects. It will encourage the Ladakhis to abandon ecologically sound methods of heat generation for an over-reliance on expensive electrical appliances and gadgetry, which they may not be able to afford and maintain in the long run.

Through the office of the D.C., the state government also provides medical services, social services, and child development and education programs. Unfortunately, the remoteness of the villages from Leh makes the delivery of these services difficult. With the increase in governmental health services, there has been a trend to treat larger numbers of patients outside the hospital.

Of special concern is the high rate of infant mortality in Ladakh. No detailed health-survey information is available, but there are an estimated 130 deaths per 1,000 births.[38] One reason for this is the severity of the winters. The infants spend their first season indoors, breathing air heavily polluted with burning animal dung. Ladakhi houses are purposely poorly ventilated, to prevent the escape of badly needed heat.

Like the Bhutanese, few Ladakhis have received sufficient education to qualify for the more important government posts. This is true in the field of education as well as civil service. As a result, technicians, administrators, consultants, and teachers are brought in from India to fill the government roles. Often these individuals have little understanding of the local culture. They do not accept the local values by which Ladakhi people live. Nor do they appreciate how the Ladakhi lifestyle maintains an ecological balance in an environment with sparse resources. The attitude of these outsiders undermines the young people's confidence in their own culture, and encourages them to develop values and behavior which will eventually erode the fabric of their society. It is expected that the employment situation will change as more Ladakhis receive college education and begin to fill the higher posts occupied by the Kashmiris.

The government of India must be given credit for all its efforts to improve the quality of life in Ladakh. Although lacking in sensitivity to many of the long-range consequences, India has conceived its various development schemes out of true concern for this fragile ecological niche. India has little to gain from providing this aid, as Ladakh possesses few if any exploitable resources.

Perhaps the greatest public service to Ladakh is currently being provided by the Ladakh Project. This small, international, nonprofit ecology group's chief mission is to stimulate meaningful social change for the Ladakhi people. Started in 1978 by Helena Norberg Hodge, a European ecologist, the Project is staffed by Ladakhis and is conceived of as an alternative development strategy. Its main goals are to educate the residents to understand the effects of development, and to suggest a variety of alternative technologies that can preserve the best of the culture while still fostering positive change in living standards.

The Project has set up an Ecological Center in Leh, where people can come to learn about the use of appropriate technology and the effects of unbridled development. The Center is staffed by a team of experts who demonstrate the various ways that people can more effectively solve their problems using local resources and available labor. The focus is on grass roots problem solving. Because of the relevance of its approach to the problems of this remote corner of India, the Center has received strong endorsements from the late Indira Gandhi, former Prime Minister Rajiv Gandhi, and His Holiness the Dalai Lama.

Before the advent of the Ladakh Project, many important resources for improving the quality of life had been untapped by the Ladakhi villagers. One resource in particular, the sun, is now being successfully exploited as a result of demonstration projects sponsored by the Ecological Center. The Ladakhis are being shown how they may use solar energy to improve heating in their homes at little cost. A demonstration project was set up in the village of Tingmosang, where "trombe walls" were added to the houses to provide heating during the freezing winter nights. These brick walls, inexpensively built onto the houses, take advantage of the strong rays of the sun during the day, storing their heat internally. After nightfall the heat is released to the rest of the house, bringing previously unimagined comfort. This heating-demonstration project was a great success, and the use of solar heating has spread to other villages in the region. The Center has also demonstrated how villagers can, at only a small cost, use the sun as a source of energy for solar water heaters, solar cookers, and solar gardening.[39]

Ladakh is once again at a major historical crossroad. Given the ever-increasing tension between the Buddhist Ladakhis and the Kashmiris, the unsettled border dispute between India and China, and the growing influence of western values and products, the inhabitants of this "Little Tibet" are deeply affected by the momentum of change. Change will come regardless, but the question is how it will come, how fast it will come and who will direct it. It will take strong and articulate indigenous leadership for Ladakh to maintain its unique identity and foster appropriate development that will both protect the culture and provide the population with a satisfying, healthy environment that can sustain the quality of life.

FOOTNOTES

1. Michael Aris, *Bhutan: The Early History of a Himalayan Kingdom* (Warminster, England: Aris & Philips Ltd., 1979).

2. *Ibid.*

3. *Ibid.*, p. 141.

4. John Avedon, *In Exile from the Land of Snows* (New York: Random House, 1984).

5. Aris, *Op. cit.*, p. 141.

6. *Bhutan: Himalayan Kingdom* (Thimpu: Bhutanese Government Publication, 1979), p. 22.

7. *Ibid.*

8. *Ibid.*

9. Leo Rose, *The Politics of Bhutan* (Ithaca: Cornell University Press, 1977).

10. Aris, *Op. cit.*, p. 151.

11. G. N. Mehra, *Bhutan: The Land of the Peaceful Dragon* (New Delhi: Vikas Publishing House, 1986), p. 49.

12. *Ibid.*

13. Bikrama J. Hasrat, *The History of Bhutan* (Thimpu: The Education Department of Bhutan, 1980), p. 49.

14. David K. Barker, *Designs of Bhutan* (Bangkok: White Lotus Co., Ltd., 1985), p. 118.

15. Brian Shaw, "Bhutan: Economy," in *The Far East and Australia—1987* (London: Europa Publications, 1986), pp. 245-246.

16. Rose, *Op. cit.*, p. 181.

17. Juliane Heyman, "Geographical Setting," in *A Survey of Nepal Society* (Berkeley: University of California Human Relations Area File, 1956), pp. 32-49.

18. Edward W. Cronin, Jr., *The Arun: A Natural History of the World's Deepest Valley* (Boston: Houghton Mifflin, 1985).

19. Haka Gurung, "Chapter Nine" (Berkeley: Nepali Conference Center for Southeast Asian Studies, 1985).

20. M. P. Malla, "Language," in P.S. Rana, ed., *Nepal in Perspective* (Kathmandu: Center for Economic Development, 1973), p. 105.

21. D. B. Bista, *The People of Nepal* (Kathmandu: Ratna Pustak Bandar, 1967).

22. *Ibid.*, ch. 3.

23. *Ibid.*

24. Jurgen Winkler, *Nepal* (Tokyo: Kodansha International, 1977).

25. For more historical background, see Rana, *Op. cit.*

26. See Introduction for more about the Indian influence on Nepalese art.

27. Prayag Sharma, "Art and Architecture," in *Nepal in Perspective* (Kathmandu: Sahayogi Press, 1972), p. 96.

28. Stella Kramrisch, *The Art of Nepal* (New York: The Asia Society, 1964), p. 27.

29. Alexander Cunningham, *Ladakh: Physical, Statistical, Historical, 1853* (New Delhi: Sagar Publications, 1977), p. 16.

30. Ferry Erdmann, "Social Stratification in Ladakh," in D. Kantowsky and S. Reihard, *Recent Research on Ladakh* (Munich: Weltform Verlag, 1981).

31. The *dzo* is a cross between a yak and a cow.

32. The Drukpa Kagyu School is the state religion of Bhutan.

33. Janet Rizvi, *Ladakh* (Delhi: Oxford Press, 1983), pp. 182–183.

34. David L. Snellgrove and Taduesz, *The Cultural Heritage of Ladakh* (New Delhi: Vikas Publishing House, 1977), pp. 23–45.

35. *Ibid.*

36. Alchi Monastery is referred to in the sections on History of Ladakh and Ladakhi Arts and Crafts.

37. Madanjeet Singh, *Himalayan Art* (New York: MacMillan, 1968), p. 54.

38. Personal communication.

39. *The Ladakh Project: Ecological Steps Towards a Sustainable Future* (New York: Open Space Institute, 1988).

BIBLIOGRAPHY
Informative Books on the Three Kingdoms

BHUTAN

Aris, Michael. *Bhutan: Early History of a Himalayan Kingdom*. Warminster, England: Aris and Philips, 1979. 344 pp.

Chakravarti, B. *A Cultural History of Bhutan*. Chandigarh: Hilltop Publishers, 1980. 138 pp.

Hasrat, Bikrama Jit. *History of Bhutan, Land of the Peaceful Dragon*. Thimpu, Education Department of the Royal Government of Bhutan, 1980. 241 pp.

Karan, Pradyumna P. *Bhutan: A Physical and Cultural Geography*. Lexington: University of Kentucky Press, 1967. 79 pp.

Karan, Pradyumna P. *Bhutan, Development amid Environmental and Cultural Preservation. Monumenta Serindica* No. 17. Institute for the Study of Languages and Cultures of Asia and Africa, 1987.

Peisel, Michael. *Lords and Lamas*. London: Heinemann Press, 1970. 180 pp.

Rathore, Laxman S. *The Changing Bhutan*. New Delhi: Jain Brothers, 1974. 186 pp.

Rose, Leo. *The Politics of Bhutan*. Ithaca: Cornell University Press, 1977.

Royal Government of the Kingdom of Bhutan Publication. *Bhutan, Himalayan Kingdom*. 1979. 48 pp.

Singh, Nagendra. *Bhutan: A Kingdom in the Himalayas*. Thompson Press Ltd., 1985. 259 pp.

Strydonck, Guy Van; Imaeda, Yoshiro; Imaeda, Francois. *Bhutan: A Kingdom in the Eastern Himalayas*. Geneva: Edition Olizane, 1984. 175 pp.

NEPAL

Bista, Bahadur. *People of Nepal*. Kathmandu: Bhotahity, 1976. 210 pp.

Fantin, Mario. *Manik Rimdu Nepal*. Singapore: Toppan Co. Ltd., 1976. 169 pp.

Fantin, Mario. *Sherpa Himalaya Nepal*. Delhi: Delhi Press, 1978. 186 pp.

Majurpuria, T.; Majurpuria, I. *Erotic Themes of Nepal*. Bangkok: Craftsman Press, 1986. 220 pp.

Maron, S.; Rose, L.; Heyman, J. *A Survey of Nepal Society*. New Haven: Human Relations Files, 1956. 313 pp.

Rana, P. S. *Nepal In Perspective*. Kathmandu: Center for Economic Development, 1973. 310 pp.

Winkler, Jurgen. *Nepal*. New York: Kodansha International, 1977. 124 pp.

LADAKH

Ahkiwalia, Major, H.F.S. *The Hermit Kingdom*. New Delhi: Vikas Publications, 1980. 186 pp.

Bedi, Rajesh; Bedi, Ramesh. *Ladakh, the Transhimalayan Kingdom*. New Delhi: Roli Books, 1981. 191 pp.

Cunningham, Alexander. *Ladakh*. New Delhi: Sagar Printers, 1953. 483 pp.

Harrer, Hans. *Ladakh*. Innsbruck: Pinguin-Verlag, 1980. 171 pp.

Johri, Major Sita Ram. *The Chinese Invasion of Ladakh*. Lucknow: Himalaya Publications, 1969. 118 pp.

Internationales Asienforum. *Recent Research on Ladakh: History, Culture, Sociology, Ecology: Proceedings*. Konstanz, Germany: Weltforum Verlag, 1983.

Ladakh Project. *Ecological Steps towards a Sustainable Future*. New York: Open Space Institute, 1988. 92 pp.

Siddiq, W.; Strom, K. *Ladakh: Between Earth and Sky*. New York: W. W. Norton, 1981. 104 pp.

Snellgrove, D.; Skorupski, T. *The Cultural Heritage of Ladakh*, Vols. 1 & 2. Delhi: Vikas Publications, 1977. 310 pp.

Sumi, Tokan. *Ladakh, the Moonland*. New Delhi: Light and Life Publications, 1977.

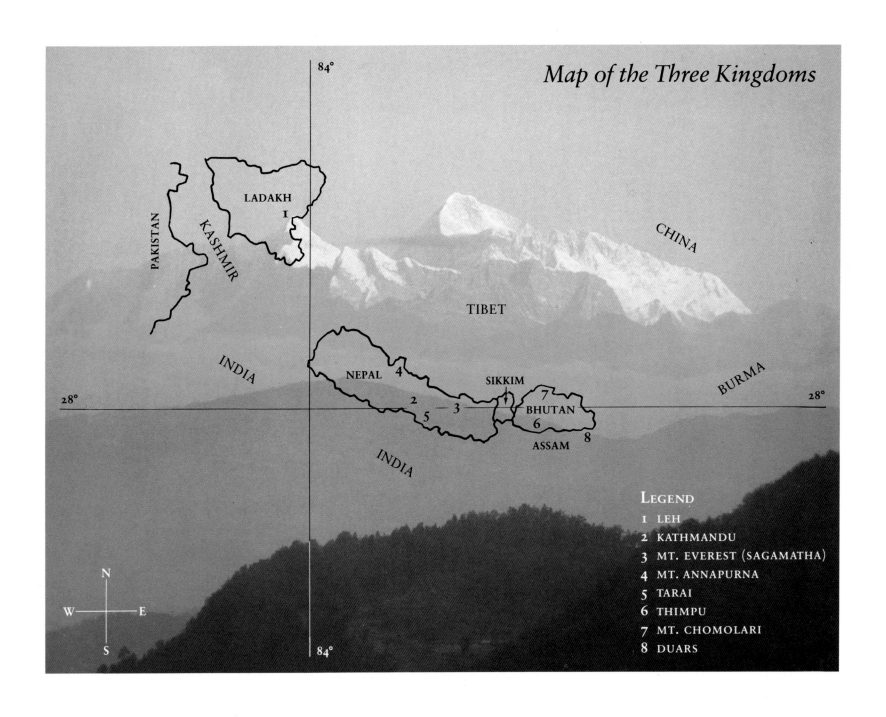

Map of the Three Kingdoms

PAKISTAN

LADAKH
1

KASHMIR

CHINA

TIBET

INDIA

NEPAL

4

SIKKIM

BURMA

2

3

7

BHUTAN

5

6

ASSAM

8

INDIA

84°

28°

28°

84°

N
W   E
S

LEGEND

1 LEH
2 KATHMANDU
3 MT. EVEREST (SAGAMATHA)
4 MT. ANNAPURNA
5 TARAI
6 THIMPU
7 MT. CHOMOLARI
8 DUARS

INDEX